I0813392

TO:

FROM:

DATE:

Self-Care
Devotions
for Teen
Girls

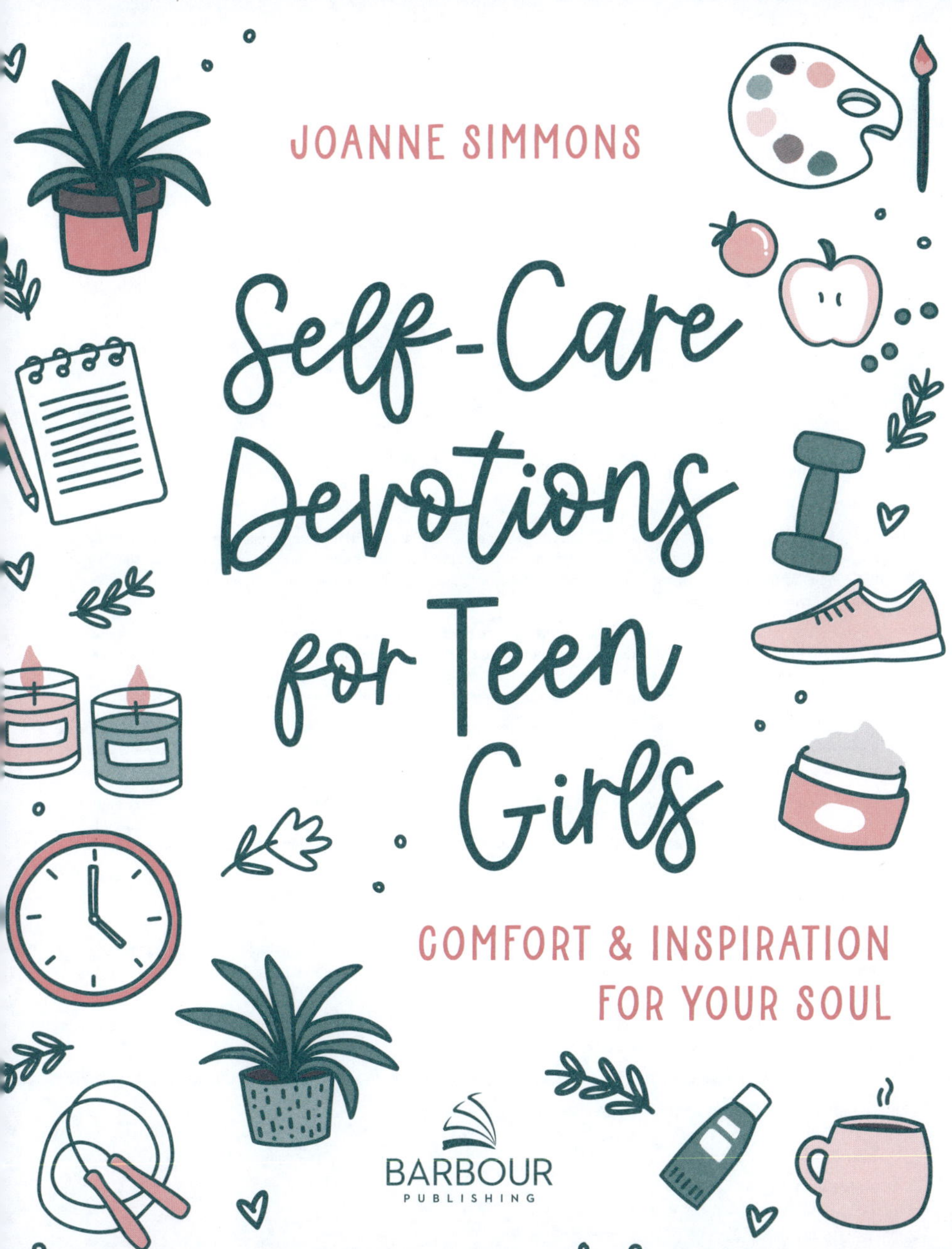

JOANNE SIMMONS

Self-Care Devotions for Teen Girls

COMFORT & INSPIRATION FOR YOUR SOUL

BARBOUR
PUBLISHING

Print ISBN 979-8-89151-215-3

Published by Barbour Publishing, Inc., 1810 Barbour Drive, Uhrichsville, Ohio 44683, www.barbourbooks.com

Our mission is to inspire the world with the life-changing message of the Bible.

Printed in China.

Introduction

Reels and stories and snaps and such might make us think we need all kinds of trendy things and comforts and cool experiences to be happy and take good care of ourselves. So it's good to remind ourselves that our *real* needs are actually pretty simple.

Do you know that God's Word has a lot to say about our true needs for self-care? And do you know that God says He will provide for those needs—but also give us so much more?

Let's do a little exploring of the Bible together through the devotions in this book. As we do, let's consider how God wants us to be intentional about total and true self-care—not just caring for our physical well-being but caring for our minds and emotions and especially our eternal spirits too! And let's focus on the very best kind of self-care—the kind where we depend fully on Jesus and His living and active Word to meet our needs and guide us, plus give us blessings piled up on top, blessings beyond our best imaginations.

How to Get Rid of Your Sin Problem, Part 1

All have sinned and fall short of the glory of God.
ROMANS 3:23 ESV

The very first step in the best kind of self-care is to get rid of your sin problem. If you've never heard, you have a sin problem. This isn't an insult. Every single person on the planet has the same problem. Here's the backstory: When God created the whole world and the first two people, Adam and Eve, He didn't make them robots programmed to love and obey Him. He gave them free will so they could *choose* to love Him and obey Him and what He designed as best for humanity. He wants love and relationship with us that are chosen and real, not forced and fake. Adam and Eve chose to disobey Him, and ever since then, sin has been spreading everywhere. And there's a big price to pay for sin—suffering and death. But God still loved people despite sin, and He knew we all would need a way for us to choose to be right with Him again (John 14:6). So He sent Jesus to be our Savior.

FATHER GOD, YOU ARE THE ONE TRUE CREATOR, AND YOU ARE PERFECT! THANK YOU FOR LOVING PEOPLE DESPITE OUR SIN PROBLEM. THANK YOU FOR SENDING YOUR SON, JESUS, AND GIVING ME AND ALL PEOPLE THE FREE WILL TO CHOOSE HIM! AMEN.

How to Get Rid of Your Sin Problem, Part 2

We are made right with God by placing our faith in Jesus Christ. And this is true for everyone who believes, no matter who we are. For everyone has sinned; we all fall short of God's glorious standard. Yet God, in his grace, freely makes us right in his sight. He did this through Christ Jesus when he freed us from the penalty for our sins. For God presented Jesus as the sacrifice for sin.

ROMANS 3:22–25 NLT

Just as Adam and Eve chose to sin, we all do. There's no way we can deny it. We all hurt others sometimes, whether intentionally or not. We act rudely. We say stupid and mean things. We have bad attitudes for no good reason. We lie or cheat in big or small ways. We gossip. We compare and get jealous. We act selfishly. The list of our sins goes on and on. But the Father who made us, the one true Creator God, has no sin. He's perfectly perfect. And we *all* need a close relationship with our Creator Father. Until we do have that close relationship, all other ways we try to be happy and take care of ourselves will ultimately never feel good enough. And the only way to have close relationship with our sinless, perfect heavenly Father is through His Son whom He sent to pay the price for our sin—Jesus Christ.

JESUS, THANK YOU SO MUCH THAT YOU MAKE IT POSSIBLE TO BE RIGHT WITH GOD AND HAVE RELATIONSHIP WITH MY HEAVENLY FATHER, THE CREATOR, BECAUSE YOU DIED ON THE CROSS TO PAY FOR MY SIN. AMEN.

How to Get Rid of Your Sin Problem, Part 3

For the sin of this one man, Adam, caused death to rule over many. But even greater is God's wonderful grace and his gift of righteousness, for all who receive it will live in triumph over sin and death through this one man, Jesus Christ.

ROMANS 5:17 NLT

Jesus willingly gave His life on the cross; He died to pay for our sin. When we admit our sin and trust in Him as the one and only Savior, we are given the most amazing gift of grace that gets rid of our sin problem! There is no better self-care than that! And when we ask Jesus to be our Savior from sin, we immediately begin relationship with our Father God. Then we can keep developing that relationship closer and closer as we allow Jesus to be Lord over our lives—and choose to follow and obey Him, learning from Him through His Word and through prayer. And the coolest bonus? We are given life that lasts forever because Jesus promised, "This is how God loved the world: He gave his one and only Son, so that everyone who believes in him will not perish but have eternal life" (John 3:16 NLT).

JESUS, I KNOW I'M A SINNER, AND I'M SORRY! I NEED YOUR FORGIVENESS AND GRACE. THANK YOU FOR DYING ON THE CROSS TO PAY THE PENALTY FOR MY SIN. THANK YOU THAT YOU ROSE TO LIFE AGAIN. THANK YOU FOR GETTING RID OF MY SIN PROBLEM AND FOR THE PROMISE OF ETERNAL LIFE. THANK YOU FOR MAKING ME RIGHT WITH GOD. I CHOOSE YOU, AND I CHOOSE TO LIVE FOR YOU! AMEN.

Your Self-Care Guide Within You

[Jesus said:] "The Helper is the Holy Spirit. The Father will send Him in My place. He will teach you everything and help you remember everything I have told you."
John 14:26 NLV

Jesus didn't leave us alone when He returned to heaven after He lived and taught during His ministry on earth and then died and rose again. He gave us the Holy Spirit. When you choose Jesus as Savior and Lord of your life, you receive the Holy Spirit directly into your life. He dwells right inside you! Think of the Holy Spirit as Your perfect, constant *true* self-care guide! (See John 16:5–15 too.)

The apostle Paul said in 1 Corinthians 6:19–20 (NLT), "Don't you realize that your body is the temple of the Holy Spirit, who lives in you and was given to you by God? . . . So you must honor God with your body." Now that you know this, think about some changes you might need to make in your self-care ideas and routines. What ways can you take care of your body better as you realize and remember that it's not just the home of your eternal soul but also the home of God's Holy Spirit? How can you honor Him by caring for yourself inside and out?

LORD, I'M SO GLAD YOU ARE ALWAYS RIGHT HERE WITHIN ME THROUGH THE PRESENCE OF THE HOLY SPIRIT. HELP ME TO CARE FOR MY BODY WELL AS YOUR DWELLING PLACE. HELP ME TO SENSE YOUR HOLY SPIRIT EVERY SINGLE MOMENT AS MY GUIDE IN EVERYTHING I DO—AND HELP ME TO LISTEN WELL TO YOUR WISDOM AND LEADERSHIP. AMEN.

The Perfect Self-Care Guidebook

All Scripture is inspired by God and is useful to teach us what is true and to make us realize what is wrong in our lives. It corrects us when we are wrong and teaches us to do what is right. God uses it to prepare and equip his people to do every good work.

2 Timothy 3:16–17 NLT

All the self-care resources in the world might have important things to share to help us take care of our bodies, minds, and emotions, but there is no better guidebook than God's written Word to us, the Bible. It's not just some ancient text. It's a living and active book (Hebrews 4:12) that communicates with us. When we read the Bible with a humble, teachable, listening attitude and talk to God through prayer, asking Him to help us learn from and follow His Word, we grow deeper in knowledge and love and faith in our heavenly Father. We grow closer to Jesus and become more aware of the Holy Spirit's presence and involvement in our lives! *Amazing!*

HEAVENLY FATHER, THANK YOU FOR THE GIFT OF THE VERY BEST SELF-CARE GUIDEBOOK—THE BIBLE. HELP ME TO LOVE YOUR WORD AND LEARN IT WELL SO THAT I GROW CLOSER TO YOU AND YOUR WILL FOR MY LIFE—AND FARTHER AWAY FROM SIN AND ITS CONSEQUENCES. AMEN.

That Fresh, Clean Feeling

[Jesus said:] "Go and make disciples of all the nations, baptizing them in the name of the Father and the Son and the Holy Spirit."
MATTHEW 28:19 NLT

You know how good a shower feels after a hot day or a lot of exercise or dirty chores. It's so nice to be washed fresh and clean and to feel brand-new again! You can think of baptism kind of like a symbol of that fresh, clean, brand-new feeling. Once you choose Jesus as Savior, it's important to be baptized. It's not something you absolutely *must* do to be saved and have forever life. (For example, the man next to Jesus on the cross never had a chance to be baptized, and Jesus promised the man he would be with Him that day in paradise. You can read about that in Luke 23.) But if you do have the opportunity, it is so awesome to obey God's Word and follow Jesus' example through baptism. It's symbolic of death to sin and of new life with Jesus. It's a way to show that you want to obey God and be like Jesus and that you are saved from sin and are His follower! And it's a wonderful testimony, example, and encouragement to others who get to witness your baptism. Here are some more passages to learn from: Acts 2:38; 22:16; 1 Peter 3:19–21.

JESUS, HELP ME TO FULLY UNDERSTAND BAPTISM AND OBEY YOU. I'M SO GRATEFUL FOR FEELING BRAND-NEW BECAUSE OF YOU, AND I WANT TO SHOW OTHERS HOW MUCH I LOVE YOU AND WANT TO LIVE MY LIFE FOR YOU. AMEN.

Total Stain Remover

"Come now, let us think about this together," says the Lord. "Even though your sins are bright red, they will be as white as snow. Even though they are dark red, they will be like wool."
ISAIAH 1:18 NLV

You might feel forever stained by sin in your life, but because of Jesus you don't have to. He can clean up any of the darkest, deepest, most stubborn stains of sin. Because of His grace, He pulls us out of the yucky muck and mire of our mistakes and helps us get back on a good clean track again. Then He works out things for our good (Romans 8:28) and for His glory so that we can share our stories with others and help them see His grace and forgiveness too. Praise Jesus for that! He's the only one who can remove the ugliest, filthiest sins and make us clean and fresh and bright again!

JESUS, I NEED YOUR MAXIMUM STAIN REMOVER—YOUR WASHED-TOTALLY-CLEAN FORGIVENESS FROM SIN! I'M SO SORRY FOR MY WRONGDOING, AND I NEED YOUR GRACE TO COVER MY SINS AND YOUR HELP TO OVERCOME THEM AND AVOID THEM IN THE FUTURE. I PRAISE YOU FOR YOUR AWESOME POWER OVER SIN AND YOUR AWESOME POWER WITHIN ME! AMEN.

Prayer Is Self-Care, Part 1

[Jesus said,] "This, then, is how you should pray."
Matthew 6:9 NIV

Prayer is self-care—put that little rhyming reminder in your brain on repeat! Prayer is your direct line of connection with the one true almighty God of the universe. Absolutely no one in all of existence is better to talk to!

If praying to God comes easily for you, that is awesome! But for some people it might be difficult. Especially if you're just starting out in your relationship with God through Jesus Christ, it might feel really awkward. But Jesus gave us a clear, straightforward example of how to pray. (You can read more about that in Matthew 6:5–15 and Mark 11:12–14, 20–26.)

First, we should spend time praising God and His holy name. We should ask for His kingdom to come and His will to be done. We should ask for our daily needs to be met. We should ask for forgiveness of our own sins, plus help and reminders to forgive others who sin against us. And we should ask for protection against temptation and sin.

Is this the only way to pray? No, but it's Jesus' specific example, and we can let it guide us every moment as we talk to God.

ALMIGHTY GOD, THANK YOU SO MUCH THAT I HAVE A DIRECT LINE TO YOU AND THAT YOU ARE ALWAYS AVAILABLE THROUGH PRAYER! PLEASE KEEP BRINGING ME BACK TO YOUR TEACHING ABOUT PRAYER TO GUIDE ME IN GOOD COMMUNICATION WITH YOU. AMEN.

Prayer Is Self-Care, Part 2

[Jesus said:] "Suppose you went to a friend's house at midnight, wanting to borrow three loaves of bread. You say to him, 'A friend of mine has just arrived for a visit, and I have nothing for him to eat.' And suppose he calls out from his bedroom, 'Don't bother me. . . .' But I tell you this—though he won't do it for friendship's sake, if you keep knocking long enough, he will get up and give you whatever you need because of your shameless persistence. And so I tell you, keep on asking, and you will receive what you ask for. Keep on seeking, and you will find. Keep on knocking, and the door will be opened to you."

LUKE 11:5–9 NLT

Now that you know a little more about prayer, don't ever, *ever* stop! Jesus taught us to keep on asking, to be persistent in prayer! As long as our requests don't go against His ways and His will, He hears us and wants to bless us with them. And if you're not sure if what you're asking Him for goes against His ways and His will, keep reading His Word daily and asking Him to show you. He is happy to answer that prayer!

LORD, I WILL KEEP ON PRAYING TO YOU! WHAT A BLESSING IT IS THAT YOU WANT ME TO! THANK YOU! AMEN.

Prayer Is Self-Care, Part 3

[Jesus said:] "Would any of you fathers give your son a stone if he asked for bread? Or would you give a snake if he asked for a fish? Or if he asked for an egg, would you give him a small animal with a sting of poison? You are sinful and you know how to give good things to your children. How much more will your Father in heaven give the Holy Spirit to those who ask Him?"

LUKE 11:11–13 NLV

Jesus continued to teach about prayer with this kind of example: If human parents who love their kids want to give good gifts to their children, how much more does our Creator, the one and only perfect loving Father, want to give us good gifts when we ask Him? If you have chosen to believe in Jesus as the Savior who paid the price for your sin, you get to be in close relationship with your heavenly Father. And His Word promises He wants to bless you with the very best kinds of gifts—and those best gifts are found through the guidance of the Holy Spirit working in your life.

LORD, THANK YOU FOR TEACHING ME ABOUT PRAYER AND GOOD GIFTS. HELP ME TO WANT THE KINDS OF GIFTS THAT ARE PERFECT FOR ME ACCORDING TO YOUR WILL. AMEN.

You Need Living Water

"Sir," the woman said, "you have nothing to draw with and the well is deep. Where can you get this living water? . . ." Jesus answered, "Everyone who drinks this water will be thirsty again, but whoever drinks the water I give them will never thirst. Indeed, the water I give them will become in them a spring of water welling up to eternal life."

JOHN 4:11–14 NIV

We all need water for self-care, that's for sure. We cannot live without it. This woman described in John 4 in the Bible was just going about her normal task of getting water at the well and had no idea she was about to have an extraordinary encounter with Jesus. He claimed to be able to give her living water—water that would become a spring welling up to eternal life. On top of that, Jesus told her how He knew everything about her. Can you imagine what she must have been thinking? Amazed, "the woman went back to the town and said to the people, 'Come, see a man who told me everything I ever did. Could this be the Messiah?'" (John 4:28–29 NIV).

JESUS, TEACH ME MORE ABOUT HOW ONLY YOU CAN OFFER THE GIFT OF LIVING WATER WELLING UP TO ETERNAL LIFE. ONLY YOU KNOW EVERYTHING. ONLY YOU CAN SAVE AND SATISFY. I TRUST IN YOU ALONE AS MY LOVING SAVIOR.

You Need the Bread of Life

Jesus then said to them, "Truly, truly, I say to you, it was not Moses who gave you the bread from heaven, but my Father gives you the true bread from heaven. For the bread of God is he who comes down from heaven and gives life to the world." They said to him, "Sir, give us this bread always." Jesus said to them, "I am the bread of life; whoever comes to me shall not hunger, and whoever believes in me shall never thirst."

JOHN 6:32–35 ESV

Do you have a favorite comfort food? A snack you consider self-care? What a blessing God has given us in so many tasty things to eat and enjoy and fill us up! But even if we could never have our favorite foods or any tasty foods ever again, we still need to eat something or we can't survive. So what was Jesus talking about in this passage? Did He mean that He expects us to believe in Him and then never eat food or drink water again? No, but Jesus does want us to trust in Him as the one who provides for all our needs. *He* is our most basic need for life because He is the giver of all life, including eternal life!

JESUS, THANK YOU FOR BEING EVERYTHING I NEED AND FOR PROVIDING EVERYTHING I NEED. I TRUST YOU, AND I WANT TO KEEP LEARNING TO TRUST YOU MORE AND MORE. AMEN.

Get Your Rest

On the seventh day God finished his work that he had done, and he rested on the seventh day from all his work that he had done. So God blessed the seventh day and made it holy, because on it God rested from all his work that he had done in creation.

GENESIS 2:2–3 ESV

Like it or not, sleep is a *huge* part of self-care. Are you getting enough? Too much? Too little? Maybe you wish you didn't need sleep at all because you have so much to do and not enough time in the day. Or maybe sleep is your favorite hobby and you'd spend a lot more time cozy in your bed if possible. Whatever the case, good rest is a blessing from God. Our minds and bodies absolutely need it, and it's important to make good time for it. Spiritually, we need it too, and we find true spiritual rest in Jesus Christ alone. He said, "Come to me, all of you who are weary and carry heavy burdens, and I will give you rest. Take my yoke upon you. Let me teach you, because I am humble and gentle at heart, and you will find rest for your souls. For my yoke is easy to bear, and the burden I give you is light" (Matthew 11:28–30 NLT).

LORD, PLEASE HELP ME TO GET GOOD AMOUNTS OF REST—PHYSICALLY, MENTALLY, AND SPIRITUALLY. THANK YOU FOR GIVING ME PEACE AND REFRESHING ME! AMEN.

Follow Jesus, Not Your Heart

Then Jesus said to his disciples, "If any of you wants to be my follower, you must give up your own way, take up your cross, and follow me. If you try to hang on to your life, you will lose it. But if you give up your life for my sake, you will save it. And what do you benefit if you gain the whole world but lose your own soul? Is anything worth more than your soul? For the Son of Man will come with his angels in the glory of his Father and will judge all people according to their deeds."

MATTHEW 16:24–27 NLT

Jesus' message in this passage is so opposite of the popular mantras of today about self-care, like "Follow your heart," "Live your truth," and "Do whatever makes you happy." To practice the best kind of self-care is to truly follow Jesus, and to truly follow Jesus means being willing to give up anything and all our own plans to say, "Your will be done with my life, Jesus—because You know and love me best." The most rewarding, most fulfilling kind of care we can get is the care Jesus wants to give when we are totally committed to Him.

JESUS, HELP ME TO REALIZE MORE AND MORE EACH DAY HOW YOU WANT TO TAKE CARE OF ME FAR BETTER THAN I COULD EVER CARE FOR MYSELF. HELP ME TO KEEP LEARNING HOW IT IS SO, SO GOOD TO TRULY FOLLOW YOU AND LIVE FOR YOU. AMEN.

Hand It Over

Give all your cares to the Lord and He will give you strength.
He will never let those who are right with Him be shaken.
PSALM 55:22 NLV

If you want to take good care of yourself, you cannot hold on to worries and fear. You have to hand them over to the Lord. Scientific studies are clear that the effects of prolonged anxiety on our minds and bodies can be serious. So learn this and then don't forget: Jesus is Lord over all your worries and fears. He promises that those who are right with Him will never be shaken. (You are right with Him when you have admitted your sin and trusted Jesus as your Savior.)

Ask yourself: What am I worried or anxious about today? What feels shaky in my life? What am I feeling unsure or fearful about? The Lord wants to take all those concerns away from you and give you peace, comfort, strength, and power instead. Call out to Him about any kind of anxiety, and then intently listen and let Him teach you how to hand it over to Him through prayer and His Word.

JESUS, I DON'T KNOW WHY I HOLD ON TO WORRIES SO OFTEN WHEN YOU'VE TOLD ME TO HAND THEM OVER TO YOU. PLEASE HELP ME GET BETTER AT GIVING YOU MY ANXIETY. I WANT TO TRUST YOU MORE AND HAVE MORE OF YOUR PERFECT PEACE AND POWER. AMEN.

Weak but Strong

[Jesus] said, "My grace is all you need. My power works best in weakness." So now I am glad to boast about my weaknesses, so that the power of Christ can work through me. That's why I take pleasure in my weaknesses, and in the insults, hardships, persecutions, and troubles that I suffer for Christ. For when I am weak, then I am strong.

2 CORINTHIANS 12:9–10 NLT

Getting good exercise is one wonderful and practical way to help with anxiety, plus it keeps our bodies healthy and strong. So evaluate how much exercise and physical activity your body is getting and how you can get some more if you need it. But be careful not to rely on it too much and get too confident in your own health and strength. Jesus does not want us to be strong on our own. That's not because He's mean and selfish. It's because He wants us to be truly strong, the best kind of strong—strong because we are depending on Him and full of His power, which never gives out and is always good.

LORD, HELP ME TO GET GOOD EXERCISE AND STRENGTH FOR MY BODY AND MIND, BUT ALSO HELP ME TO BE HAPPY TO BE WEAK ON MY OWN—BECAUSE THAT MEANS I MUST GET REAL STRENGTH FROM YOU. REMIND ME THAT I'M ONLY TRULY STRONG WHEN I'M CHOOSING TO DEPEND ON YOU FOR EVERYTHING. THANK YOU FOR WANTING THE VERY BEST FOR ME. THANK YOU FOR FILLING ME WITH YOUR POWER AND LOVE. AMEN.

Exercise Your Faith

[Jesus said,] "Blessed are all who hear the word of God and put it into practice."
LUKE 11:28 NLT

Even better than exercising our bodies for self-care is exercising our faith. It's easy to fail to actually *do* anything with what we are learning about following God's Word. If we're not careful, we could read or listen to God's Word all day every day and choose not to let it change or motivate us in any way.

Jesus knew this is something we all struggle with sometimes, and He emphasized that we're blessed when we both hear God's Word *and* put it into practice. The Bible also teaches this in James 1:22–25 (NLT): "Don't just listen to God's word. You must do what it says. Otherwise, you are only fooling yourselves. For if you listen to the word and don't obey, it is like glancing at your face in a mirror. You see yourself, walk away, and forget what you look like. But if you look carefully into the perfect law that sets you free, and if you do what it says and don't forget what you heard, then God will bless you for doing it."

LORD, HELP ME TO TRULY EXERCISE MY FAITH AND WHAT I'M LEARNING ABOUT YOU AND YOUR WORD. HELP ME TO DO THE GOOD THINGS YOU WANT AND GET RID OF THE THINGS YOU DON'T WANT IN MY LIFE. AMEN.

Renew Every Thought

Take hold of every thought and make it obey Christ.
2 CORINTHIANS 10:5 NLV

Your mind needs constant care and protection. We live in a world with many people who don't love Jesus, and sometimes we spend too much time focusing on what they do and say and think—especially through TV, movies, and social media—and soon it seems that the world's ideas are filling our minds. We might start to copy and maybe even affirm trends that go against God's ways and His Word. If that's happening, we need a renewal of our minds, and we can ask Jesus for help as we seek to take hold of every one of our thoughts and make them obey Him. The Bible says, "Do not act like the sinful people of the world. Let God change your life. First of all, let Him give you a new mind. Then you will know what God wants you to do. And the things you do will be good and pleasing and perfect" (Romans 12:2 NLV).

JESUS, PLEASE HELP ME TO CARE FOR AND PROTECT MY MIND WELL. REMIND ME THAT MUCH THAT THE WORLD OFFERS ME IS HARMFUL—EVEN THINGS THAT SEEM GOOD AND FINE AND HARMLESS AT FIRST. HELP ME TO TAKE EVERY THOUGHT I HAVE AND REFOCUS IT ON YOU AND THE GOOD THINGS YOU WANT FOR MY LIFE! AMEN.

Our One and Only Savior

Jesus is holy and has no guilt. He has never sinned and is different from sinful men. He has the place of honor above the heavens. Christ is not like other religious leaders. They had to give gifts every day on the altar in worship for their own sins first and then for the sins of the people. Christ did not have to do that. He gave one gift on the altar and that gift was Himself. It was done once and it was for all time.

HEBREWS 7:26–27 NLV

There are many options for what the world might call "spiritual self-care" these days. There are all kinds of beliefs and religions. And maybe you have heard someone say all religions and spiritual practices are the same, so just pick whatever seems to fit your personality. However, if you spend even a little time learning about some of the other religions and beliefs, you realize they are all quite different, and how can they all be true? If everything is true, then nothing can be true. It's chaos! There must be one ultimate source of truth.

Belief in Jesus as God and as our one and only Savior is the one true religion, and it is explained through studying God's Word, the Holy Bible. Jesus alone was (and is) perfect and holy and without sin. He suffered and died to pay the price for our sin and then rose again and offers salvation and eternal life to all people of all time. They need only to admit their sin and trust in Him. No other religion offers that kind of miracle and that awesome gift of love and mercy!

LORD JESUS, THERE TRULY IS NO ONE ELSE LIKE YOU! YOU ALONE ARE WORTHY OF MY FAITH. YOU ARE GOD AND YOU ARE THE ONE TRUE SAVIOR! AMEN.

Go to Church

Let us hold tightly without wavering to the hope we affirm, for God can be trusted to keep his promise. Let us think of ways to motivate one another to acts of love and good works. And let us not neglect our meeting together, as some people do, but encourage one another, especially now that the day of his return is drawing near.

HEBREWS 10:23–25 NLT

Even once you're solidly believing that the Christian faith in Jesus Christ is the one true religion, you have so many churches and types of churches and even online churches to pick from. But ask God to give you His wisdom and help You understand more about being actively involved in a solid, true Bible-teaching church. God's Word tells us that we need to meet regularly with other Christians who trust Jesus as their Savior. We need to worship and learn more about God together, and we need to encourage one another, comfort one another, and take good care of one another!

LORD, PLEASE GIVE ME WISDOM ABOUT THE IMPORTANCE AND PURPOSE OF BEING PART OF A CHURCH THAT TEACHES YOUR WHOLE WORD AND TRULY HONORS YOU. THANK YOU FOR ALL THE OTHER CHRISTIANS WHO ARE IN MY LIFE AND IN LOCAL CHURCHES—AND ALSO FOR THE ONES ALL OVER THE WORLD, YOUR GLOBAL CHURCH! HELP US TO LOVE GETTING TOGETHER AT CHURCH TO GROW CLOSER TO YOU AND TO ONE ANOTHER. AMEN.

Make Your Life Really Rich

Let the teaching of Christ and His words keep on living in you. These make your lives rich and full of wisdom.
COLOSSIANS 3:16 NLV

We need to be rich to have the best self-care—but not the kind of "rich" the world might make you think of. We need to be rich like Colossians 3:16 describes—rich because we let the teaching of Jesus Christ and His words keep on living in us. If we do that—meaning we focus on, listen to, and obey Jesus' teaching and example—we will have lives that are *really* rich and full of wisdom. Not necessarily a life full of money and possessions and luxuries, but for sure a life overflowing with all the goodness God wants to give us—especially the things money can never buy. So as you make choices about how you self-care and what you allow and put into your life and mind, you can ask yourself, *Does this help me to focus on honoring and following Jesus and His teaching or not?* If not, what could I choose instead that would help me focus on Him and obey His teaching more?

JESUS, HELP ME TO BE RICH LIKE YOU WANT ME TO BE—WITH A WONDERFUL LIFE FULL OF YOUR WISDOM AND BLESSINGS BECAUSE I LET YOU LEAD AND LOVE ME. AMEN.

Beware of Greed

[Jesus] said, "Beware! Guard against every kind of greed. Life is not measured by how much you own."
LUKE 12:15 NLT

Having good self-control over your social media habits is super important for self-care. A big problem with social media is that it stirs up jealousy and greed in us. We all struggle with those feelings sometimes anyway, even if we spend no time on social media. So constantly scrolling and staring at pictures and posts about what everyone else has and is doing has huge potential to create even more feelings of jealousy and greed in us. And Jesus strongly warned us about that. We have to be on guard to keep our thoughts and desires fixed on what Jesus wants for us and to be content with the blessings He has already given and will continue to give according to His perfect will and timing for our lives.

LORD, IT'S SO EASY TO LOOK AT THE LIVES OF OTHERS AND WANT WHAT THEY HAVE RATHER THAN SIMPLY TO BE CONTENT WITH MY OWN LIFE AND BLESSINGS THAT YOU'VE ALREADY GIVEN ME. SO PLEASE HELP ME TO BE CAREFUL ABOUT COMPARISON AND JEALOUSY AND GREED. I WANT TO REMEMBER YOUR GOOD WARNINGS. AMEN.

Don't Get Caught Up in Appearances

Don't be concerned about the outward beauty of fancy hairstyles, expensive jewelry, or beautiful clothes. You should clothe yourselves instead with the beauty that comes from within, the unfading beauty of a gentle and quiet spirit, which is so precious to God.

1 PETER 3:3–4 NLT

Of course it's part of self-care to want to look our best. We enjoy looking nice and finding cute outfits and doing our makeup. But we need to be careful not to get caught up in physical appearance. Because no matter what anyone tries to tell you or what social media tries to show you, authentic beauty comes from the inside, not what anyone looks like on the outside. Your heart—the way you treat others and share God's kindness and love in the ways His Word teaches—is what makes you truly gorgeous. If you have a gentle and quiet spirit, it means you are listening for God's voice and leading in your life and you put your hope in Him. That's the kind of beauty that never fades and never goes out of style.

LORD, PLEASE HELP ME NOT TO GET CAUGHT UP IN APPEARANCE. I WANT TO FOCUS ON REAL, AUTHENTIC INNER BEAUTY THAT SHINES OUTWARD AND HELPS OTHERS WANT TO KNOW YOU AS SAVIOR! AMEN.

Don't Be Lazy

Do not be lazy but always work hard.
Work for the Lord with a heart full of love for Him.
ROMANS 12:11 NLV

We certainly need rest and relaxation for good self-care, but we also need to work hard! Look up these various verses on laziness: Proverbs 12:24; 13:4; 2 Thessalonians 3:10; 1 Timothy 5:8, just to name a few!

So, what is your work ethic like? Are you willing to work hard? Do you do your very best with the gifts and talents God has given you? A good work ethic doesn't mean you should never rest or have fun—that time is necessary too! But it's easy to get lazy and have too much rest and too much fun. Think of the Lord as the manager overseeing you in any task you do, because ultimately, He is! But He's the best kind of manager—full of love and blessing for you as you do the good work He created you for (see Ephesians 2:10).

JESUS, I WANT TO HAVE A WORK ETHIC THAT SHOWS OTHERS I WORK TO HONOR YOU MOST OF ALL. PLEASE HELP ME TO GIVE MY BEST EFFORT AND FIND JOY IN MY WORK NO MATTER WHAT IT IS. YOU ARE SO GOOD TO ME, AND I'M HONORED TO DO MY BEST FOR YOU! AMEN.

Avoid It!

I will set no sinful thing in front of my eyes. I hate the work of those who are not faithful. It will not get hold of me. A sinful heart will be far from me. I will have nothing to do with sin.

PSALM 101:3–4 NLV

You need to avoid sin as much as possible if you want to practice good self-care. It's no easy task, for sure, because the world loves to make sin look good and fun and harmless. So we can let the writer of Psalm 101 inspire us. He made a big promise in this passage. It was easier in his time to make that promise because there were no movies and TV shows, smartphones, or social media back then. So these days we have to be extra careful about what we look at and pay attention to because the world is so full of sinful things available at all times in all places—and our enemy the devil wants to push every sinful thing on us so that we will walk away from following Jesus.

DEAR LORD, I WANT TO MAKE THIS PROMISE TOO—I DON'T WANT TO LOOK AT OR WATCH ANYTHING THAT IS SINFUL. I WANT TO AVOID SIN AS MUCH AS POSSIBLE, AND I SURE NEED YOUR POWERFUL HELP! AMEN.

A Good Dose of Scripture

Every word of God has been proven true.
He is a safe-covering to those who trust in Him.
PROVERBS 30:5 NLV

Memorizing scripture is so, so powerful for your mental self-care! God loves to bring verses you have learned to your mind exactly when you need them. Sometimes the most calming scriptures, like Psalm 23, can help you to relax your breathing when you feel panicky. Sometimes singing praises like Psalm 136 are exactly what you need to have joy instead of the fear creeping up on you. Sometimes powerful scripture that recounts the faith of others and the miracles of God, like Hebrews 11, is exactly what you need to grow your faith that God can do a miracle in your situation too. Keep filling your mind with God's Word every chance you get and see how He uses it to guide you, care for you, and protect you!

HEAVENLY FATHER, PLEASE CARE FOR ME IN DETAILED WAYS THROUGH A GOOD DOSE OF YOUR WORD. PLEASE BRING SPECIFIC VERSES AND PASSAGES TO MY MIND EXACTLY WHEN I NEED THEM TO KEEP MY FOCUS FIXED ON YOU! AMEN.

Make Goals and Go After Them

We can make our plans,
but the Lord determines our steps.
Proverbs 16:9 NLT

God has made us with many cool abilities and gifts and talents to use. So we need to make good goals for our lives and go after them! But as we make them, we need to ask Jesus what His will is and be willing to change our plans if He shows us that we should. He will determine each of our steps—and even if it's hard sometimes, we need to willingly accept that. Sometimes His steps for us will match exactly what we hoped for, and sometimes He might want to teach us something along a totally different way than what we wanted. But when we humbly follow Jesus anywhere He says to go, He is going to lead us along the very best paths and plans for our lives. Proverbs 3:5–6 (NIV) says, "Trust in the Lord with all your heart and lean not on your own understanding; in all your ways submit to him, and he will make your paths straight."

DEAR LORD, I WANT TO TRUST YOU MORE THAN MYSELF. PLEASE HELP ME TO MAKE GOOD GOALS AND GO AFTER THEM BUT ALSO BE WILLING TO CHANGE MY PLANS AS YOU SEE FIT. HELP ME TO HUMBLY LET YOU LEAD, BECAUSE I LOVE YOU AND I KNOW YOU WILL ALWAYS TAKE THE BEST CARE OF ME. AMEN.

You Need Strong Roots

I fall to my knees and pray to the Father, the Creator of everything in heaven and on earth. I pray that from his glorious, unlimited resources he will empower you with inner strength through his Spirit. Then Christ will make his home in your hearts as you trust in him. Your roots will grow down into God's love and keep you strong. And may you have the power to understand, as all God's people should, how wide, how long, how high, and how deep his love is. May you experience the love of Christ, though it is too great to understand fully. Then you will be made complete with all the fullness of life and power that comes from God.

EPHESIANS 3:14–19 NLT

To be a truly strong young woman, you need real, eternal strength that comes from Jesus. As you trust in Him, He makes His home in your heart, and you grow stronger every day that you continue to choose Him. Like a tree with good roots, you won't be knocked over and broken during the storms of life.

DEAR LORD, I WANT TO BE ROOTED STRONGLY AND SECURELY IN YOU. HELP ME TO FOCUS ON HOW UNSURPASSABLE AND ENDLESS YOUR LOVE IS FOR ME! AND HELP ME TO KEEP INCREASING IN STRENGTH EVERY DAY WITH YOU IN MY HEART. AMEN.

You Can Overcome

Children, you belong to God, and you have defeated these enemies. God's Spirit is in you and is more powerful than the one who is in the world. These enemies belong to this world, and the world listens to them, because they speak its language. We belong to God.

1 JOHN 4:4–6 CEV

♡

Some people like to brag that they're never afraid of anything. But don't believe them. We all get scared or anxious or worried about something occasionally. True bravery and courage come from admitting fears and worries and facing them anyway. Bravery isn't possible unless you first know that you fear something but then decide to deal with it. And sometimes you deal with things so well that you totally overcome them—and then they're never a fear or worry again! With God's Holy Spirit working in you to help, you can face anything and overcome it. Jesus said, "I have told you these things, so that in me you may have peace. In this world you will have trouble. But take heart! I have overcome the world" (John 16:33 NIV).

DEAR LORD, I CAN'T DENY THAT I HAVE FEARS AND WORRIES SOMETIMES, AND I SURE NEED YOUR HELP TO FACE THEM. I BELIEVE WHOLEHEARTEDLY THAT YOU CAN HELP ME OVERCOME THEM. AMEN.

God Loves in Great Detail

[Jesus said,] "Are not two sparrows sold for a penny? Yet not one of them will fall to the ground outside your Father's care. And even the very hairs of your head are all numbered. So don't be afraid; you are worth more than many sparrows."

MATTHEW 10:29–31 NIV

You know best how you like to take care of your hair and style it—whether you like to take your time and try new products and styles or you're a fuss-free kind of girl. But not even you could ever possibly count the hairs on your head. But God certainly can! He created You and loves with a super-detailed kind of love. Jesus taught that there is no one who knows and loves you like your heavenly Father does. God cares about everything in His creation, even the tiniest of birds, but He knows and loves people most of all—and that includes you!

DEAR JESUS, THANK YOU FOR TEACHING ME THAT GOD KNOWS ME EVEN BETTER THAN I KNOW MYSELF—AND LOVES ME RIGHT DOWN TO THE TINIEST DETAILS. HELP ME TO FOCUS ON THAT TRUTH AND NEVER FORGET IT! AMEN.

Retail Therapy

[Jesus said,] "Don't store up treasures on earth! Moths and rust can destroy them, and thieves can break in and steal them. Instead, store up your treasures in heaven, where moths and rust cannot destroy them, and thieves cannot break in and steal them. Your heart will always be where your treasure is."

MATTHEW 6:19–21 CEV

Sometimes some of us need a little "retail therapy" for self-care. Can you relate? But we need to be wise about it, because all the things we can shop for and own in this world are nice, for sure—like clothes and jewelry and makeup and decor and the fun things we collect. And it's okay to enjoy those things as long as we don't worship them—making it our main goal and motivation to get more stuff. Nothing on this earth lasts forever. Things break or get old or end up lost. Entertainment and vacations come to an end. You can't take your stuff to heaven with you when your life on earth is over. So Jesus taught us to store up treasure in heaven. That's where our blessings last forever. And how do we store up treasure in heaven? We ask God to show us the good works He has planned for us to do, and we love and follow and obey Him.

DEAR LORD, HELP ME TO FOCUS MORE ON WHAT YOU TAUGHT ABOUT TREASURE IN HEAVEN RATHER THAN GAINING TREASURES HERE ON EARTH. AMEN.

Spend Time in Worship

Make a joyful noise to the Lord, *all the earth! Serve the* Lord *with gladness! Come into his presence with singing! Know that the* Lord, *he is God! It is he who made us, and we are his; we are his people, and the sheep of his pasture. Enter his gates with thanksgiving, and his courts with praise! Give thanks to him; bless his name! For the* Lord *is good; his steadfast love endures forever, and his faithfulness to all generations.*

Psalm 100 ESV

Being super intentional about spending time in praise and worship to our awesome God is one of the best forms of self-care. Do you need to be more intentional about it? You might need to put your phone down more often to make time. You might need to stop stressing over studying for a bit to make time. You might need to tell your friends you need some alone time with God. Whatever the case, you need to make and keep good plans worshipping and bowing before God regularly. Psalm 46:10 (ESV) says, "Be still, and know that I am God. I will be exalted among the nations, I will be exalted in the earth!" Focus on God's qualities and His creation and tell Him how awesome He is and how grateful you are for His goodness.

AWESOME GOD, I WORSHIP YOU ALONE, AND EVERY DAY I WANT TO FOCUS MORE ON HOW INCREDIBLE YOU ARE! I AM DELIGHTED AND AMAZED BY YOU! NO ONE ELSE IS LIKE YOU! I PRAISE YOU, AND I'M SO GRATEFUL TO BE LOVED AND KNOWN BY YOU! AMEN.

Be a Generous, Cheerful Giver

"Bring all the tithes into the storehouse so there will be enough food in my Temple. If you do," says the Lord *of Heaven's Armies, "I will open the windows of heaven for you. I will pour out a blessing so great you won't have enough room to take it in! Try it! Put me to the test! Your crops will be abundant, for I will guard them from insects and disease. Your grapes will not fall from the vine before they are ripe," says the* Lord *of Heaven's Armies. "Then all nations will call you blessed, for your land will be such a delight," says the* Lord *of Heaven's Armies.*

MALACHI 3:10–12 NLT

Being a generous, cheerful giver *to others* might not seem like a form of *self*-care, but it is. Through the prophet Malachi, God encouraged the people of Israel to see how much He would bless them when they were obedient in giving their tithes and offerings to Him. We can remember this in our own lives. God loves it when we give cheerfully (2 Corinthians 9:7). And Jesus said, "Give, and you will receive. Your gift will return to you in full—pressed down, shaken together to make room for more, running over, and poured into your lap. The amount you give will determine the amount you get back" (Luke 6:38 NLT).

LORD, HELP ME TO BE CHEERFULLY GENEROUS. PLEASE REMIND ME OF YOUR PROMISES OF BLESSING WHEN I OBEY YOUR GOOD COMMANDS. AMEN.

Keep Tough Skin

Dear friends, don't be surprised at the fiery trials you are going through, as if something strange were happening to you. Instead, be very glad— for these trials make you partners with Christ in his suffering, so that you will have the wonderful joy of seeing his glory when it is revealed to all the world. If you are insulted because you bear the name of Christ, you will be blessed, for the glorious Spirit of God rests upon you.

1 PETER 4:12–14 NLT

Take good care to keep yourself tough-skinned against insults for being a strong Christian. Loving and following Jesus means, yes, you probably will be insulted if you're doing your best to follow Him and obey God's Word. What's cool and popular in the world is often opposite of what God's Word says is good and right. And when you don't go along with what's cool and popular, there's a good chance you'll be ridiculed, insulted, and made fun of. That's not easy, but you can handle it. You are tough and brave because of the power of God's Holy Spirit within you. Our almighty God promises to bless you, and His Spirit never, ever leaves you.

DEAR LORD, PLEASE KEEP ME TOUGH-SKINNED AND HAPPY TO BE CALLED A CHRISTIAN NO MATTER WHAT ANYONE ELSE SAYS ABOUT ME. WHAT YOU THINK ABOUT ME MATTERS MORE THAN ANYTHING. YOU MAKE ME STRONG AND BRAVE, AND YOU FILL MY LIFE WITH BLESSINGS. AMEN.

So Refreshing

At one time we thought of Christ merely from a human point of view. How differently we know him now! This means that anyone who belongs to Christ has become a new person. The old life is gone; a new life has begun!
2 CORINTHIANS 5:16–17 NLT

Sometimes we feel like we need to be totally refreshed somehow, yet with something so much better than just a vacation or a spa day or a mani-pedi. It's like we need a whole new start and a new mindset. So it's *so good* to remember that with Jesus as our Savior we have become new creations, and He blesses us with endless newness by His grace when we have gotten caught up in and then stuck in and weighed down by the things of the world. For "if we confess our sins, he is faithful and just to forgive us our sins and to cleanse us from all unrighteousness" (1 John 1:9 ESV), and His mercies are new every morning (Lamentations 3:22–23).

DEAR LORD, THANK YOU FOR REFRESHING ME! PLEASE HELP ME TO REMEMBER THAT I AM A NEW CREATION BECAUSE I'VE ASKED YOU TO BE MY SAVIOR. I WANT TO LIVE WITH TOTAL JOY AND CONFIDENCE AS I REMEMBER THAT YOU CLEANSE ME FROM SINS WHEN I CONFESS THEM TO YOU, AND YOU GIVE ME NEWNESS EVERY SINGLE DAY. AMEN.

Take Care with Good Relationships

God loves you and has chosen you as his own special people. So be gentle, kind, humble, meek, and patient. Put up with each other, and forgive anyone who does you wrong, just as Christ has forgiven you. Love is more important than anything else. It is what ties everything completely together. Each one of you is part of the body of Christ, and you were chosen to live together in peace. So let the peace that comes from Christ control your thoughts. And be grateful.

COLOSSIANS 3:12–15 CEV

Relationships with friends and family can be messy and full of mistakes that we are all guilty of making sometimes. But relationships are an absolute necessity in life. We all need to help take good care of one another in all kinds of ways. And so—since we are God's loved and chosen special people because we're trusting and following Jesus as our Savior—we need to remember this scripture and let love, gentleness, kindness, humility, meekness, patience, gratitude, and the peace that comes from Jesus control our minds and hearts and actions toward others—just like we need others to do that back toward us too.

DEAR LORD, PLEASE HELP ME HAVE AND MAINTAIN GOOD RELATIONSHIPS WITH FAMILY AND FRIENDS. FILL US WITH ALL THE PEACE AND GOODNESS THAT COME FROM YOU—AND HELP US ALL TO TRULY TAKE CARE OF ONE ANOTHER IN EVERY WAY. AMEN.

Your Best Relationship

*See what great love the Father has lavished on us,
that we should be called children of God! And that is what we are.*
1 JOHN 3:1 NIV

It's so wonderful and so necessary to have earthly family and friends, but it's even better to know we are in the family and friendship of the one true almighty God. Sometimes troubles in earthly families and friendships get totally out of control. Relationships end, and earthly families might even totally break apart. It's terribly sad, and so, being part of God's family is especially important because we know that no matter what goes on in earthly relationships, we are always God's children and *no one* can break that bond. And with the one true almighty God as our loving Father, we have all His care and protection every single day of our lives.

DEAR JESUS, YOU ARE MY BEST AND MOST IMPORTANT RELATIONSHIP. I'M SO THANKFUL THAT BECAUSE OF YOU AND HOW YOU DIED TO SAVE ME FROM SIN, I'M A CHILD OF ALMIGHTY GOD, WHO LOVES ME AND TAKES GOOD CARE OF ME—TODAY, TOMORROW, AND FOREVER. AMEN.

Gather and Pray

[Jesus said,] "For where two or three gather together as my followers, I am there among them."
MATTHEW 18:20 NLT

Who are the people you share your most personal needs and concerns and worries with? Yes, we can and should share everything with God through prayer, but we need people to help carry our burdens too (Galatians 6:2). We need to spend time praying together and helping one another. If you don't do this already, start a regular prayer time with the people you love ASAP! While at home or church or school or your activities, offer to pray for your family and friends, and ask them to pray for you too. Find creative, smart, and efficient ways and times to share needs and join together in prayer. Prayer is powerful, and gathering together to support one another with prayer brings about more of its benefits and power in our lives.

DEAR JESUS, I'M SO GRATEFUL THAT PEOPLE CAN GATHER AND PRAY TO YOU ANYTIME, ANYWHERE, AND YOU ARE WITH US! THANK YOU FOR FAMILY AND FRIENDS WHO JOIN WITH ME BEFORE YOU. THANK YOU FOR THE TIMES THAT ARE SO ENCOURAGING AS WE FOCUS ON YOU AND BRING OUR PRAISE AND NEEDS TO YOU. AMEN.

Good and Healthy Friendships

Walk with the wise and become wise; associate with fools and get in trouble. Trouble chases sinners, while blessings reward the righteous.
PROVERBS 13:20–21 NLT

Are you taking good care of yourself regarding the *quality* of your friendships? Healthy friendships are so good for us. But some friendships can be really bad for us. The friends who love and trust Jesus as Savior and encourage us (1 Thessalonians 5:11) in our walk with Him are such a needed and special blessing! But the friends who don't love Jesus require caution. Of course we should want to have some friends who are nonbelievers so that hopefully we can help lead them to salvation in Jesus at some point. But we never want them to lead us away from Jesus with a stronger influence on us than we have on them. God's Word says bluntly that "bad company corrupts good character" (1 Corinthians 15:33 NIV).

DEAR JESUS, PLEASE BLESS ME WITH GOOD FRIENDS WHO LOVE YOU LIKE I DO. HELP ME TO BE CAREFUL WITH FRIENDS WHO DON'T LOVE AND TRUST YOU AS THEIR SAVIOR. I WANT TO HELP LEAD THEM TO YOU, BUT I NEVER WANT THEM TO PULL ME AWAY FROM YOU. AMEN.

Morning and Night Routines

On my bed I remember You. I think of You through the hours of the night. For You have been my help. And I sing for joy in the shadow of Your wings. My soul holds on to You. Your right hand holds me up.
PSALM 63:6–8 NLV

Let me hear Your loving-kindness in the morning, for I trust in You. Teach me the way I should go for I lift up my soul to You.
PSALM 143:8 NLV

What are your morning and evening self-care routines? As you're readying for the day or brushing your teeth before bed, think about ways you can include time with God. Like these passages from Psalms describe, ask the Lord to tell you about His unfailing love each morning. Ask Him to show you the good choices to make in your day—and to avoid the bad. Let Him lead you on the right path and teach you to do His will.

Then, make another goal to spend time with God every night as part of your bedtime routine too. The important thing is that you regularly praise God and pray to Him, listen to Him, and learn from Him.

DEAR LORD, I WANT TO BEGIN AND END MY DAYS WITH YOU—AND THINK OF AND LISTEN TO YOU ALL THROUGHOUT THE DAY TOO. PLEASE KEEP ME CLOSE TO YOU AND HELP ME TO FOLLOW THE GOOD THINGS YOU HAVE PLANNED FOR ME. AMEN.

Take Good Care of Your Reputation

A good name is to be chosen instead of many riches. Favor is better than silver and gold. The rich and the poor meet together. The Lord is the maker of them all. A wise man sees sin and hides himself, but the foolish go on, and are punished for it. The reward for not having pride and having the fear of the Lord is riches, honor and life.

PROVERBS 22:1–4 NLV

Are you taking good care of your reputation? When people hear your name, what do they probably think? Do you want them to think of you in good ways or bad? Do you want to be known for things like laziness or lying or cheating or being snobby or rude? Or do you want to be known for things like doing your best and being honest, fair, kind, compassionate, and worthy of respect? What does God's Word say you should want? When you live for God and follow His ways of real love and kindness and integrity, you will make and keep a good name for yourself. Best of all, you will bring glory and honor to Him!

DEAR LORD, I WANT TO HAVE AND KEEP A GOOD REPUTATION. PLEASE HELP ME TO TAKE GOOD CARE OF IT AND, MOST IMPORTANTLY, POINT OTHERS TO KNOWING YOU AS THE ONE TRUE GOD AND JESUS AS OUR ONE AND ONLY SAVIOR. AMEN.

Remind Yourself That You Are Never Alone

"She will give birth to a son, and they will call him Immanuel, which means 'God is with us.'"
MATTHEW 1:23 NLT

Sometimes the best self-care you need is just a solid reminder that you aren't alone. The Bible promises that it's truly impossible to be alone: "Where can I go from Your Spirit? Or where can I run away from where You are? If I go up to heaven, You are there! If I make my bed in the place of the dead, You are there! If I take the wings of the morning or live in the farthest part of the sea, even there Your hand will lead me and Your right hand will hold me" (Psalm 139:7–10 NLV). God is with you through His Spirit *at all times*. And you can let the fact that Jesus came to earth as a human remind you that He understands your human struggles. You can feel seen and understood and loved and cared for because of your Savior! Jesus wants to help and guide and protect you anytime and anywhere.

DEAR JESUS, IMMANUEL, YOU ARE HERE RIGHT NOW AND ALWAYS THROUGH THE HOLY SPIRIT. YOU UNDERSTAND ME SO WELL. PLEASE HELP ME TO TRUST YOU, DEPEND ON YOU, AND RELATE TO YOU MORE EACH DAY. REMIND ME THAT I AM ALWAYS LOVED AND NEVER ALONE. AMEN.

Accept the Hard Realities

"Blessed are those who trust in the Lord and have made the Lord their hope and confidence. They are like trees planted along a riverbank, with roots that reach deep into the water. Such trees are not bothered by the heat or worried by long months of drought. Their leaves stay green, and they never stop producing fruit."

Jeremiah 17:7–8 NLT

It's good for us just to know how to accept the hard realities of life. And one of those hard realities is that people let us down sometimes. There's no person on earth who is perfect. Yes, God thankfully blesses us with trustworthy people—but even the most reliable person on earth can't be 100 percent reliable. They're always capable of disappointing or hurting us, intentionally or not, because they are human and have a sin nature. We need and are grateful for good people relationships, but even better is to seek God above all and put our full trust in Him, knowing that our most important relationship is with Him. He alone is perfectly reliable and worthy of our full trust and full praise.

LORD, I TRUST IN YOU MORE THAN ANYONE ELSE. YOU GIVE ME CONFIDENCE AND STRENGTH BECAUSE YOU ARE THE STEADFAST ROCK THAT I CAN DEPEND ON AND BUILD MY LIFE ON. AMEN.

Protection from the Enemy, Part 1

Watch out for your great enemy, the devil. He prowls around like a roaring lion, looking for someone to devour. Stand firm against him, and be strong in your faith.
1 PETER 5:8–9 NLT

Protecting yourself from and fighting off a deadly enemy is of course good self-care. And unfortunately we all have a deadly enemy—the devil, described in the Bible like a roaring lion looking to destroy and devour us. We need to be alert and have courage to stand against and fight him. We can only do that by staying close to God—through reading His Word, praying continually, and being involved in a Bible-teaching church that helps us grow closer to our heavenly Father who can always protect us. We have to keep godly habits and have good friendships with people who encourage and support us in our faith. And we have to be very careful to keep distance from people and anything that might lead us away from God. The devil wants to steal from, kill, and destroy us (John 10:10) by getting us off alone or using bad influences to tempt us into disobeying and rejecting God and His Word. But we can stand up to our enemy and fight with the power God gives us!

DEAR GOD, PLEASE HELP ME TO STAY ALERT FOR THE DEVIL AND BE READY TO FIGHT HIM IN YOUR POWER. HELP ME TO BE SELF-PROTECTIVE AND MOST OF ALL TO KEEP MYSELF UNDER YOUR PROTECTION. AMEN.

Protection from the Enemy, Part 2

The One Who lives in you is stronger than the one who is in the world.
1 John 4:4 NLV

Our enemy the devil is eagerly stirring up all kinds of evil in this world. And you will be under attack from him and from the power of sin sometimes, in all sorts of different ways—through someone else's unkind words or actions, through stressful times for your family, through painful times of loss, through sickness, and on and on. You can probably make a list right now, unfortunately. But no matter how strong the enemy and his evil seem, the devil is never stronger than the power of God in you through the Holy Spirit—all because you love and trust in Jesus as your Savior.

DEAR JESUS, I FORGET THE TRUTH SOMETIMES THAT YOU ARE ALWAYS STRONGER THAN ANY EVIL ATTACK AGAINST ME, ANY HARD THING I'M GOING THROUGH. PLEASE REMIND ME AND FILL ME WITH YOUR STRENGTH AND POWER THROUGH THE HOLY SPIRIT. AMEN.

God's Perfect Protection and Shelter

Live under the protection of God Most High and stay in the shadow of God All-Powerful. Then you will say to the Lord, "You are my fortress, my place of safety; you are my God, and I trust you." The Lord will keep you safe from secret traps and deadly diseases. He will spread his wings over you and keep you secure. . . . The Lord Most High is your fortress. Run to him for safety, and no terrible disasters will strike you or your home. God will command his angels to protect you wherever you go. They will carry you in their arms.

Psalm 91:1–4, 9–12 CEV

These are such awesome promises from God's Word! For the best kind of self-care, we want to live under the perfect protection and in the shelter of the one true almighty God. So how do we do that? First, we trust Him as the one true God. We believe in Jesus as our only Savior. We do our best to follow God's Word and obey and do what it says. We stay in close relationship with our heavenly Father. All of that is awesome anyway, plus we receive many gifts of God's care on top!

DEAR GOD, THANK YOU FOR YOUR AWESOME PROMISES ABOUT YOUR PROTECTION OF ME IN PSALM 91! I WANT TO STAY IN YOUR PROTECTION EVERY DAY OF MY LIFE.

Be Sincere

[Jesus said]: "When you pray, do not be as those who pretend to be someone they are not. They love to stand and pray in the places of worship or in the streets so people can see them."

MATTHEW 6:5 NLV

Take good care of yourself by being a sincere person. That might sound a lot like being *serious*, but it doesn't mean you can't have fun and be silly sometimes and have a great sense of humor. It means you want to be *genuine*, and the good things you do on the outside match real goodness going on inside your mind and heart. It means you don't do things just to be a show-off.

Jesus gave an example of how to be sincere when we pray—*not* in a way that draws attention to ourselves and tries to make us look good. Our prayers should be real conversation, a time of praise and asking our Lord for His help and learning from Him.

In all our words and actions, we need to be careful not to be show-offs who point to ourselves as the center of attention. We should constantly want to put others' attention on the one who deserves all praise—our one true almighty God, who is Father, Son, and Holy Spirit!

ALMIGHTY GOD, IN EVERYTHING I DO, HELP ME TO BE A SINCERE AND GENUINE PERSON. HELP ME TO POINT PEOPLE TO YOU AS THE ONE WORTHY OF ALL ATTENTION. AMEN.

Be Full of Real Joy, Part 1

This is the day that the Lord has made.
Let us be full of joy and be glad in it.
PSALM 118:24 NLV

Joy is essential for self-care, and we must choose joy, remind ourselves of joy, look for joy, focus on joy—all the joy things!—every day of our lives. Some days feel like there is absolutely nothing good in them. Big and little things go wrong, and we feel discouraged and defeated. But while things may feel awful, God's Word doesn't change based on our feelings. And His Word says, "This is the day that the Lord has made. Let us be full of joy and be glad in it." We can find reasons for joy in the midst of anything—especially when we remember the best reason for joy is that nothing can separate us from God's love or take away the eternal life that He gives us when we trust in Jesus Christ alone as Savior.

DEAR JESUS, I WANT TO HAVE JOY NO MATTER WHAT IS GOING ON IN MY LIFE. REMIND ME EVERY MOMENT THAT REAL JOY DOESN'T FADE WITH EARTHLY CIRCUMSTANCES. REAL JOY COMES FROM YOU, AND I TRUST YOU TO FILL ME WITH IT! AMEN.

Be Full of Real Joy, Part 2

Though you have not seen [Jesus Christ], you love him;
and even though you do not see him now, you believe in him
and are filled with an inexpressible and glorious joy, for you are
receiving the end result of your faith, the salvation of your souls.
1 PETER 1:8–9 NIV

Happy feelings come and go in this life and depend on so many different factors. But for those who love and follow Jesus as Savior, real joy—inexpressible and glorious joy!—comes from knowing and trusting Him. We know that we are saved from our, sin and that eternal confidence is incredible! We can keep coming back to God's Word daily to let scripture stir up real joy inside us every single day.

DEAR JESUS, REMIND ME THAT TEMPORARY HAPPINESS IS NOT THE SAME AS ETERNAL, DEEP-DOWN JOY. I PRAISE AND THANK YOU FOR THE INEXPRESSIBLE AND GLORIOUS JOY YOU FILL ME WITH INSIDE BECAUSE I KNOW I AM LOVED AND SAVED BY YOU! AMEN.

A Reason to Celebrate?

[Jesus said,] "God blesses you when people mock you and persecute you and lie about you and say all sorts of evil things against you because you are my followers. Be happy about it! Be very glad! For a great reward awaits you in heaven."

MATTHEW 5:11–12 NLT

We need good, fun celebrations in our lives, but Jesus tells us to celebrate something unusual—the instances when we're mocked and persecuted in all kinds of ways for following Him. *What?* It's really hard to think of those as a blessing and reason to party! However, God hears each instance, He's keeping track, and He rewards loyalty and love for Him. If you're ever made fun of or hurt or lied about because you follow Jesus, remember this scripture. Then trust that Jesus knows every moment you suffer for Him, and He will bless you in wonderful ways and make everything right one day.

DEAR JESUS, HELP ME TO STAY POSITIVE EVEN UNDER PERSECUTION. REMIND ME THAT YOU SAY TO CELEBRATE THE HARD TIMES I SUFFER FOR YOU—BECAUSE YOU SEE AND WILL BLESS ME FOR STAYING LOYAL TO YOU.

Deal with the Hard and Sad

Has the Lord rejected me forever? Will he never again be kind to me? Is his unfailing love gone forever? Have his promises permanently failed? Has God forgotten to be gracious? Has he slammed the door on his compassion? . . . But then I recall all you have done, O Lord; I remember your wonderful deeds of long ago. They are constantly in my thoughts. I cannot stop thinking about your mighty works.

Psalm 77:7–9, 11–12 NLT

Sometimes it's tempting to want to avoid hard things and think only happy, easy thoughts and seek out only fun times. But real self-care deals with the hard and sad things so that we don't push them down and deny them, resulting in them being bottled up so much that one day they explode.

God can handle all our hard thoughts and questions. It's okay to ask Him about them and show Him all our emotions about them. Maybe you're struggling with rejection, sadness, or pain, or all of those right now, just like the writer of this psalm was. Sometimes in the midst of something awful, we wonder where Jesus is and if He has forgotten to take care of us. So we need to focus well on remembering all the good things He has done for us in the past, in His perfect timing, and trust that He will continue.

DEAR LORD, PLEASE BE NEAR AND COMFORT ME AND GIVE ME YOUR PERFECT WISDOM WHILE I ASK YOU THESE HARD QUESTIONS. PLEASE DRAW ME CLOSE AND HELP ME TO REMEMBER YOUR TRUTH, GOODNESS, AND LOVE. AMEN.

The Most Important Rules for Life

"Teacher, which one is the greatest of the Laws?" Jesus said to him, "'You must love the Lord your God with all your heart and with all your soul and with all your mind.' This is the first and greatest of the Laws. The second is like it, 'You must love your neighbor as you love yourself.' All the Laws and the writings of the early preachers depend on these two most important Laws."
MATTHEW 22:36–40 NLV

Through Jesus' teaching, the one true God gave us the two most important rules for all of life. Since He is the Creator of each of us plus the entire universe, that's definitely something we should listen to and obey if we want to take good care of ourselves! Jesus said the two most important commandments to obey are to love God first with all your heart, soul, and mind—and to love your neighbor as yourself. If we focus on obeying these commandments, we will automatically do other things well too. Sometimes you'll hear people say something like, "Jesus just says to love everyone. That's all you have to do." But they ignore the fact that Jesus said before we love others, we are to love God first and most of all. We can't love others in the best ways that God intended unless we first love God with all our hearts, souls, and minds—and that includes getting to know Him through His Word and through prayer.

DEAR GOD, ABOVE ALL ELSE, I WANT TO OBEY THESE GREAT COMMANDMENTS YOU GAVE. PLEASE HELP ME TO STAY FOCUSED ON THEM EVERY DAY. I WANT TO HONOR YOU! AMEN.

Don't Try to Get Even

Don't mistreat someone who has mistreated you. But try to earn the respect of others, and do your best to live at peace with everyone. Dear friends, don't try to get even. Let God take revenge. In the Scriptures the Lord says, "I am the one to take revenge and pay them back."

ROMANS 12:17–19 CEV

Sometimes the best way to take care of ourselves when we've been mistreated is just to back away and let God handle it. It's super hard to do, but God loves us much more than we can possibly imagine. We can trust Him to take care of our needs and bring justice when we've been wronged. That doesn't mean we have to be weak and allow ourselves to be walked on. That doesn't mean God never asks us to do something to stand up for ourselves. It means we humbly ask for God's help and His plans for true justice more than anything else. We ask Him to guide us and tell us when to speak up and when to be quiet, when to act and when to be still. God knows and sees everything, and He gets angry at injustice too! His justice and goodness will always prevail, not always in the timeline we'd like but always according to His perfect schedule.

DEAR GOD, SHOW ME WHEN I NEED TO BACK AWAY WHEN I'VE BEEN MISTREATED AND I'M UPSET. PLEASE CALM ME DOWN AND GUIDE ME. HELP ME TO LET YOU HANDLE ISSUES WITH YOUR PERFECT JUSTICE AND TIMING. AMEN.

Get and Give Forgiveness

Peter came to Jesus and asked, "Lord, how many times shall I forgive my brother or sister who sins against me? Up to seven times?" Jesus answered, "I tell you, not seven times, but seventy-seven times."
MATTHEW 18:21–22 NIV

We all need to get forgiveness from others sometimes—and give it too. Those can be hard conversations, but they're essential to taking good care of ourselves and our relationships. And we need God's grace and forgiveness most of all! Because of Jesus' work on the cross to pay for our sin, God is never stingy with forgiveness. He's extremely generous with it, and He taught us to be too. When Jesus' disciple Peter asked for a specific number of times he should forgive someone sinning against him, Jesus answered in a way that means that whatever amount we first think is right, we should go way above and beyond that amount—because, through Jesus, God goes way above and beyond at loving and forgiving us! That's an incredible blessing to be grateful for, and we should want to share that blessing.

DEAR LORD, PLEASE HELP ME TO DO MY BEST AT FORGIVING OTHERS IN ABOVE-AND-BEYOND KINDS OF WAYS LIKE YOU FORGIVE SO GENEROUSLY. THANK YOU, THANK YOU, THANK YOU! AMEN.

Don't Play with Sin

Happy is the man who does not walk in the way sinful men tell him to, or stand in the path of sinners, or sit with those who laugh at the truth. . . . For the Lord knows the way of those who are right with Him. But the way of the sinful will be lost from God forever.

PSALM 1:1, 6 NLV

Especially in your teenage and young adult years, the world will tell you how fun it is to play around with sin and risky behavior. But do you want to believe that lie, or do you truly want to take good care of yourself? Because God's Word tells you to run away from the evil desires of youth and pursue righteousness, faith, love, and peace instead (2 Timothy 2:22). Watch even a few minutes of the daily news. Do you want to trust the crazy, broken world and dabble in sin, or do you want to trust the never-changing God who gives you life and your every breath and who loves You so much He even gave His only Son to die for you?

DEAR LORD, PLEASE HELP ME TO STAND STRONG IN MY LOVE FOR YOU, MY FAITH IN YOU, AND MY OBEDIENCE TO YOU NO MATTER WHAT CRAZY THING THE WORLD IS TELLING ME IS HARMLESS AND JUST FOR FUN. REMIND ME OF YOUR DEEP LOVE AND GREAT SACRIFICE TO PAY FOR MY SIN SO THAT I WILL NEVER WANT TO PLAY AROUND WITH SIN. AMEN.

Confession Is Key

If we say we have no sin, we deceive ourselves, and the truth is not in us. If we confess our sins, he is faithful and just to forgive us our sins and to cleanse us from all unrighteousness.

1 JOHN 1:8–9 ESV

Confessing sin is a huge key to good self-care. Sin has bad consequences, and we can't rid it from our lives unless we're admitting it to God and asking for His forgiveness and then His help to avoid more of it in the future. He is all-knowing, and He hears our thoughts and prayers—every single one. But if we truly want Him to listen and answer us, we need always to admit our sins, not hold on to them. The Bible promises that God forgives us and removes our sin as far as the east is from the west (Psalm 103:12), but first we need to confess those sins. That keeps us humble and depending on Jesus and His saving grace, which is the very best self-care—to be dependent on the one who loves us so much He was willing to die for us.

DEAR JESUS, IT WOULD BE CRAZY TO TRY TO HIDE MY SIN FROM YOU. THESE ARE THE SINS I'VE BEEN STRUGGLING WITH: ________. PLEASE FORGIVE ME FOR THEM AND REMOVE THEM FROM ME. THANK YOU THAT YOU DO. I WANT TO DEPEND ON YOU, AND I NEED YOUR MERCY AND GRACE EVERY MOMENT! AMEN.

Trust in the Lord with All Your Heart

Trust in the LORD with all your heart and lean not on your own understanding; in all your ways submit to him, and he will make your paths straight. Do not be wise in your own eyes; fear the LORD and shun evil. This will bring health to your body and nourishment to your bones.

PROVERBS 3:5–8 NIV

Even though so many messages and themes you hear these days will tell you to trust your heart and follow your dreams, that's not always the best advice. Before you do, make sure your heart and your dreams match up with what Jesus wants for you. So often we're tempted and motivated by what is sinful and bad for us. So God's Word tells us to trust Him with all our hearts and not to lean on our own understanding. We need to stay close to Him through reading His Word, praying, worshipping Him, and serving Him. We can trust Him to make straight paths for our dreams when they match up with His perfect plans for our lives.

JESUS, I WANT TO TRUST IN YOU MORE THAN I TRUST IN MYSELF. PLEASE LEAD ME ON STRAIGHT PATHS. IF I STRAY AWAY FROM YOU, PLEASE HELP ME REALIZE IT IMMEDIATELY AND QUICKLY GET BACK TO FOLLOWING YOU CLOSELY! AMEN.

A Big Choice During Hard Times

[Jesus said,] "I have told you these things, so that in me you may have peace. In this world you will have trouble. But take heart! I have overcome the world."
JOHN 16:33 NIV

It's sad that it's true, but it's a very broken world. All kinds of awful things can happen to us or people we know. But in the middle of any hard thing, everyone has a very important choice to make. (It's a choice because God will never force us to love and obey Him. He wants our real love out of our own free will.) In difficulty and pain, will we choose to get closer to God or further away? Will we choose to let Him help and comfort or choose to hold on to anger and blame Him for all difficulty and pain? The wise choice is to grow closer to Him. Psalm 34:17–18 (NLV) says, "Those who are right with the Lord cry, and He hears them. And He takes them from all their troubles. The Lord is near to those who have a broken heart."

DEAR LORD, PLEASE HELP ME NEVER TO GROW FURTHER FROM YOU WHEN MY HEART FEELS BROKEN AND I'M HURTING AND CONFUSED. I WANT TO DRAW CLOSER TO YOU AS I REMEMBER YOUR LOVE AND THAT YOU WANT TO HEAL MY BROKEN HEART. AMEN.

Don't Get Down on Yourself

"There's a young boy here with five barley loaves and two fish. But what good is that with this huge crowd?" "Tell everyone to sit down," Jesus said. So they all sat down on the grassy slopes. (The men alone numbered about 5,000.). . . After everyone was full, Jesus told his disciples, "Now gather the leftovers, so that nothing is wasted." So they picked up the pieces and filled twelve baskets with scraps left by the people who had eaten.

JOHN 6:9–10, 12–13 NLT

Don't ever get down on yourself or think you don't have enough or aren't enough. Let the story of Jesus working a miracle through a young boy and his lunch encourage and inspire you! Jesus did an amazing thing when He took that little lunch and fed a huge crowd of people with many baskets left over. Think about how many of those people must have believed in Jesus that day after seeing such a stunning miracle! Let this inspire you to be faithful even if you are ever feeling small or insignificant. Who knows how Jesus will bless and show you miracles because of your generosity and obedience to Him, even in ways that might seem so small?

DEAR LORD, REMIND ME THAT I'M NEVER INSIGNIFICANT. I AM LOVED AND SAVED FOREVER BY YOU, AND YOU CREATED ME WITH PERFECT PLANS! PLEASE TAKE WHAT I HAVE TO OFFER AND TURN IT INTO SOMETHING MUCH BIGGER FOR YOUR GLORY! AMEN.

God Is with You, Holding You Up

So do not fear, for I am with you; do not be dismayed,
for I am your God. I will strengthen you and help you;
I will uphold you with my righteous right hand.
ISAIAH 41:10 NIV

Have you ever been so sick or in so much pain that you couldn't even hold yourself up, let alone try to take good care of yourself? Maybe someone had to carry you or let you lean on them. In those moments, that is God's love given to you via the people who are helping. When you look back and think about those hard times and who God provided to help, you can look forward and not be afraid of anything that might happen today or in the future. You can trust that God will provide exactly the people and things you need to deal with any difficulty or heartache that is to come.

DEAR GOD, THANK YOU FOR THE WAYS YOU PROVIDE FOR ME THROUGH PEOPLE WHO LOVE AND CARE FOR ME WHEN I CAN'T TAKE CARE OF MYSELF. THANK YOU FOR ENCOURAGING ME, STRENGTHENING ME, AND HELPING ME WITH EVERYTHING. THANK YOU FOR HOLDING ME UP. AMEN.

Be Humble and Serve Others

After Jesus had washed his disciples' feet. . .he said: Do you understand what I have done? You call me your teacher and Lord, and you should, because that is who I am. And if your Lord and teacher has washed your feet, you should do the same for each other. I have set the example, and you should do for each other exactly what I have done for you. I tell you for certain that servants are not greater than their master, and messengers are not greater than the one who sent them. You know these things, and God will bless you, if you do them.

JOHN 13:12–17 CEV

Jesus is King of kings and Lord of lords. Everyone on earth will bow down to Him one day. He could be full of pride, but He isn't. He is truly a humble servant-leader, and He showed an example of that when He washed His disciples' feet. Then He taught that they should do the same and that they would be blessed for being humble servants of one another. That message was not just for the disciples; it's for us today too!

DEAR JESUS, THANK YOU FOR SHOWING US HOW TO BE HUMBLE AND HOW TO SERVE AND LOVE OTHERS. I WANT TO BE LIKE YOU AND TREAT OTHERS LIKE YOU DO. AMEN.

Unchanging While Things Are Changing

Jesus Christ is the same yesterday and today and forever.
HEBREWS 13:8 NLV

You go through lots of change while you're young, and it's good to expect change all your life, and to be resilient and flexible. That will help your mental self-care. Some people get too caught up in wanting things to always stay the same, and they make life extra stressful for themselves. Change is inevitable. That's why we can be so thankful that God gave us Jesus, who is always dependable and always the same—yesterday, today, and forever! Psalm 102:25–27 (NLV) says, "You made the earth in the beginning. You made the heavens with Your hands. They will be destroyed but You will always live. They will all become old as clothing becomes old. You will change them like a coat. And they will be changed, but You are always the same. Your years will never end."

Jesus is *never* going to let you down. So lean on Him and ask Him to hold you steady when life seems crazy. Talk to Him about all your joys and all your fears and all your needs.

DEAR JESUS, WHILE LIFE IS ALWAYS CHANGING, THANKS FOR BEING UNCHANGING. YOU ARE MY CONSTANT, STEADY SOURCE OF TRUTH, LOVE, WISDOM, AND DIRECTION.

Seek and Find God

"For I know the plans I have for you, declares the Lord, *plans for welfare and not for evil, to give you a future and a hope. Then you will call upon me and come and pray to me, and I will hear you. You will seek me and find me, when you seek me with all your heart."*

Jeremiah 29:11–13 ESV

Sometimes we wish Jesus were physically right here, right now in our present day, to teach and love us in person. Thankfully we do have the Holy Spirit's presence with us, and we have God's Word to teach and guide us. We have God's promises that we can find Him (Deuteronomy 4:29), and He is never far from us (Acts 17:27). If we ever feel that God is far away or we can't find Him, we need to look at what our attitudes and actions and habits have been lately. Have we been holding on to any sin we need to let go of and seek forgiveness for? Have we been spending regular time with God through His Word and in prayer? James 4:8 (NLT) says, "Come close to God, and God will come close to you. Wash your hands, you sinners; purify your hearts, for your loyalty is divided between God and the world."

DEAR GOD, THANK YOU THAT I CAN SEEK AND FIND YOU. YOU'RE NOT HIDING. YOU WANT TO BE FOUND AND YOU WANT TO BE CLOSE TO ME. HELP ME TO GET RID OF ANYTHING IN MY LIFE THAT CREATES DISTANCE FROM YOU. AMEN.

Take Care and Don't Give Up

Be patient, then, brothers and sisters, until the Lord's coming. See how the farmer waits for the land to yield its valuable crop, patiently waiting for the autumn and spring rains. You too, be patient and stand firm, because the Lord's coming is near. . . . Brothers and sisters, as an example of patience in the face of suffering, take the prophets who spoke in the name of the Lord. As you know, we count as blessed those who have persevered. You have heard of Job's perseverance and have seen what the Lord finally brought about. The Lord is full of compassion and mercy.

JAMES 5:7–8, 10–11 NIV

We just feel like giving up sometimes, but we have to be so careful not to. The Christian life has many hard challenges, and it's understandable and common to grow weary of doing the right thing and believing and following the one true God and His Word—especially in a world that increasingly rejects Him. But as this scripture reminds us, the Lord is full of compassion and mercy. He cares, and He sees our faithfulness. We can look back to examples of those who have persevered before us and were greatly blessed, like Job, and be encouraged to keep going strong and be faithful as we follow Jesus and wait for His return.

DEAR JESUS, WITH YOUR HELP, I WON'T GIVE UP ON LOVING AND FOLLOWING YOU. I BELIEVE IN YOU AND YOUR PROMISES AND BLESSINGS. AMEN.

Hold Your Head High

The Lord will be your confidence.
Proverbs 3:26 esv

One way to take good care of your mental and emotional health is by not letting embarrassing or awkward moments hurt your self-esteem. We've all been there, done that in so many kinds of ways. If we're not careful, the weird/humiliated feelings can live on in our minds endlessly. But the embarrassment is usually a much bigger deal to us than anyone else. We might want to melt into the floor or wish to be invisible, but when we remember Proverbs 3:26 we can hold our heads high instead. God is our confidence through all our problems and challenges, both big and small.

DEAR LORD, REMIND ME WHERE MY REAL CONFIDENCE COMES FROM—YOU! PLEASE COMFORT ME AND HELP ME WHEN I'M FEELING EMBARRASSED AND AWKWARD. THANK YOU FOR LOVING ME NO MATTER WHAT. AMEN.

Keep Your Mouth Shut, Part 1

Watch your tongue and keep your mouth shut, and you will stay out of trouble.
PROVERBS 21:23 NLT

Taking good care of ourselves sometimes means keeping our mouths shut. God's Word is pretty blunt about being careful with what we say. We all know that it's hard to control our tongues. We talk back and give insults and tease too much sometimes. It's especially challenging to watch our words when we're angry or upset or feeling hurt or mistreated by someone. So it's important to focus on scripture passages like the following that remind us of the benefits of choosing words carefully.

> *Some people make cutting remarks, but the words of the wise bring healing. (Proverbs 12:18 NLT)*
>
> *"If you want to enjoy life and see many happy days,*
> *keep your tongue from speaking evil and your lips from telling lies." (1 Peter 3:10 NLT)*
>
> *A gentle tongue is a tree of life, but a sinful tongue crushes the spirit. (Proverbs 15:4 NLV)*

DEAR LORD, PLEASE SET A GUARD OVER MY MOUTH AND WATCH OVER THE DOOR OF MY LIPS (PSALM 141:3). I WANT TO BE CAREFUL WITH MY WORDS AND HONOR YOU WITH THEM. AMEN.

Keep Your Mouth Shut, Part 2

Let the words of my mouth and the thoughts of my heart be pleasing in Your eyes, O Lord, my Rock and the One Who saves me.

PSALM 19:14 NLV

So, when you're doing well and controlling your tongue and you've held back all those words you wanted to say but didn't, what do you do with them? It's not good to bottle them up and let them turn into internal anxiety. So give them to God! Remember that He already knows them anyway (Psalm 139:4). Vent to Him about all your frustrated and angry feelings. He tells us in His Word to give all our anxiety to Him because He cares for us (1 Peter 5:7). He wants us to pray about everything (Philippians 4:6), and we can ask Him to trade the angry and awful words we want to say for His peace and positivity instead. We can let Him give us wisdom to know what words to say and when to say them when we find ourselves in conflict and difficult conversations.

DEAR LORD, HELP ME TO REMEMBER TO KEEP MY MOUTH SHUT AND TALK TO YOU ABOUT ALL THE THINGS I WANT TO SAY BUT SHOULDN'T. PLEASE GIVE ME PEACE AND WISDOM TO KNOW WHAT TO SAY AND WHEN I SHOULD SAY IT. AMEN.

Be Ready to Face Temptation

Then Jesus was led by the Spirit into the wilderness to be tempted there by the devil. For forty days and forty nights he fasted and became very hungry. During that time the devil came.
MATTHEW 4:1–3 NLT

Satan wants to tempt us to sin and suffer the consequences. By reading the whole account of Jesus' temptation by Satan in Matthew 4, we can learn how to be ready to face Satan and similar temptation. It shows us how dangerous he can be. He will do anything to try to destroy us and make us turn away from obeying God. He knows scripture too and might even twist it to try to confuse us or take it out of context to get us to sin. Lots of people in our world also work in those same kinds of ways to try to turn us away from Jesus. We have to keep asking Jesus for protection and wisdom and strength to stand up against Satan's lies and ploys. And ultimately we must tell him the same thing Jesus told him: "Get out of here, Satan. . . . For the Scriptures say, 'You must worship the LORD your God and serve only him'" (Matthew 4:10 NLT).

DEAR JESUS, HELP ME TO BE STRONG AGAINST SATAN'S LIES AND EVIL TACTICS LIKE YOU WERE. I WORSHIP AND SERVE YOU ALONE! AMEN.

Clean and Ready for Good Work

In a wealthy home some utensils are made of gold and silver, and some are made of wood and clay. The expensive utensils are used for special occasions, and the cheap ones are for everyday use. If you keep yourself pure, you will be a special utensil for honorable use. Your life will be clean, and you will be ready for the Master to use you for every good work. Run from anything that stimulates youthful lusts. Instead, pursue righteous living, faithfulness, love, and peace. Enjoy the companionship of those who call on the Lord with pure hearts.

2 TIMOTHY 2:20–22 NLT

It takes a whole lot of self-control and self-care to stay pure and to run away from sin in this messed-up world. But this scripture passage encourages you to do so. Think about how you want God to use your life. Do you want to be just like regular everyday wood and clay, or do you want to be like shining gold used for better purposes? When you work hard to live a clean life, as far away from sin as possible, God can use you for the very best things He has planned.

DEAR LORD, EVERY DAY PLEASE SHOW ME WHAT AREAS OF MY LIFE NEED TO BE PURIFIED. HELP ME TO STAY FAR AWAY FROM THE SINFUL THINGS THAT ARE BAD FOR ME. USE MY LIFE IN THE WONDERFUL WAYS YOU CREATED ME FOR. AMEN.

Want Wisdom and Use Wisdom, Part 1

Joyful is the person who finds wisdom, the one who gains understanding. For wisdom is more profitable than silver, and her wages are better than gold. Wisdom is more precious than rubies; nothing you desire can compare with her. She offers you long life in her right hand, and riches and honor in her left. She will guide you down delightful paths; all her ways are satisfying. Wisdom is a tree of life to those who embrace her; happy are those who hold her tightly.

PROVERBS 3:13–18 NLT

Lots of the world's self-care techniques involve ways to avoid looking old and gray, yet wisdom is often thought of as old and gray, not young and trendy. But no matter what the world says is popular, it's truly a much-needed gift to be wise—to be able to judge right from wrong and use caution and good sense and stay away from sin. You can be wise right now, even as a teen. God's Word says, "If any of you lacks wisdom, you should ask God, who gives generously to all without finding fault, and it will be given to you" (James 1:5 NIV). There's no age requirement in that scripture, so ask God to give you wisdom, and then use it and see all the blessings that come your way.

DEAR GOD, PLEASE GIVE ME LOTS OF YOUR PERFECT WISDOM! I BELIEVE WHAT YOUR WORD SAYS ABOUT ITS BENEFITS AND BLESSINGS. PLEASE HELP ME TO INSPIRE OTHERS MY AGE TO WANT YOUR WISDOM AND TO USE IT IN THEIR LIVES TOO. AMEN.

Want Wisdom and Use Wisdom, Part 2

But when you ask, you must believe and not doubt, because the one who doubts is like a wave of the sea, blown and tossed by the wind. That person should not expect to receive anything from the Lord. Such a person is double-minded and unstable in all they do.

James 1:6–8 NIV

To take good care of ourselves, it's important to remember not just to ask God for His wisdom and leave it at that. Once you ask for wisdom, you can be full of faith and fully expect God to give wisdom as He has promised. Then you need to use that wisdom to make your decision or take your next step or stay out of trouble or run away from sin—whatever your situation calls for. If we're doubtful toward God and His wisdom, we become wishy-washy and unsteady, and we're easily tossed around by bad advice or the popular ideas of this world—and that comes with a strong warning that we'll never receive blessings from God.

DEAR LORD, I DON'T WANT TO DOUBT YOU. I WANT TO USE THE WISDOM AND GUIDANCE YOU GIVE ME. I WANT TO BE STRONG AND CONFIDENT IN YOU. PLEASE HELP ME TO STAND FIRM IN MY FAITH. AMEN.

No Shame as You Shine

"You are the light of the world—like a city on a hilltop that cannot be hidden. No one lights a lamp and then puts it under a basket. Instead, a lamp is placed on a stand, where it gives light to everyone in the house. In the same way, let your good deeds shine out for all to see, so that everyone will praise your heavenly Father."
MATTHEW 5:14–16 NLT

You are the light of the world, carrying the best news to share, and you don't ever need to let anyone make you feel ashamed for loving and following Jesus. With the Holy Spirit living inside you, your job is to shine your light that points to Jesus so that others will want to trust Him as Savior and praise God too! We should never want to dim or hide our light. So many people in the dark world around us sure do need the good news and love of Jesus, so we need to shine as brightly as possible, saying boldly, "I am not ashamed of this Good News about Christ. It is the power of God at work, saving everyone who believes" (Romans 1:16 NLT).

DEAR JESUS, I WANT TO BE BOLD ABOUT SHARING THE GOSPEL NO MATTER WHAT PEOPLE THINK. HELP ME TO SHINE BRIGHTLY, WITH NO SHAME, TO POINT PEOPLE TO YOU! THANK YOU FOR WANTING TO SAVE ALL PEOPLE FROM THEIR SINS! AMEN.

Stay Joined to the Gardener

I am the true vine, and my Father is the gardener.
JOHN 15:1 CEV

Plants need good care to grow and thrive, and so do we. Jesus used an example of a grapevine to show us how we can produce fruit—meaning how we can do good things in our lives for God's glory—and to help us understand how God cares for us:

> *Stay joined to me, and I will stay joined to you. Just as a branch cannot produce fruit unless it stays joined to the vine, you cannot produce fruit unless you stay joined to me. I am the vine, and you are the branches. If you stay joined to me, and I stay joined to you, then you will produce lots of fruit. But you cannot do anything without me. If you don't stay joined to me, you will be thrown away. You will be like dry branches that are gathered up and burned in a fire. Stay joined to me and let my teachings become part of you. Then you can pray for whatever you want, and your prayer will be answered. (John 15:4–7* CEV*)*

DEAR LORD, I WANT TO STAY JOINED TO YOU AND LET YOU TAKE GOOD CARE OF ME. THANK YOU FOR HEARING MY PRAYERS AND HELPING ME GROW AND THRIVE. AMEN.

Lift Up Your Eyes

I will lift up my eyes to the mountains. Where will my help come from? My help comes from the Lord, Who made heaven and earth. He will not let your feet go out from under you. He Who watches over you will not sleep. Listen, He Who watches over Israel will not close his eyes or sleep. The Lord watches over you. The Lord is your safe cover at your right hand. The sun will not hurt you during the day and the moon will not hurt you during the night. The Lord will keep you from all that is sinful. He will watch over your soul. The Lord will watch over your coming and going, now and forever.

Psalm 121 NLV

The best way to take good care of your eyes spiritually is to keep them lifted up, always looking to God for help and hope. What are you needing His help for today? It can be anything! Sometimes it's the smaller things, even just help finding your missing cell phone. Sometimes it's big things like struggling with illness or dealing with friendship trouble or grieving over the loss of a loved one. Or maybe you feel unsafe and like you desperately need protection. Almighty God promises both to help you and to keep you safe, and you can trust Him to keep that promise. Cry out to Him and lift your eyes, watching and waiting patiently for Him to come to your rescue in various ways and through various people.

DEAR LORD, MY EYES ARE LIFTED UP TO YOU. THANK YOU FOR YOUR HELP AND PROTECTION IN EVERY SITUATION. I'M SO GRATEFUL TO BE YOUR CHILD, NOW AND FOREVER. AMEN.

When You Need Total Healing

They ran throughout that whole region and carried the sick on mats to wherever they heard [Jesus] was. And wherever he went—into villages, towns or countryside—they placed the sick in the marketplaces. They begged him to let them touch even the edge of his cloak, and all who touched it were healed.

MARK 6:55–56 NIV

Jesus had all power back in Bible times to heal people, and He still has that power today. So if you need healing, pray and trust that it is absolutely possible for you to receive a miracle. But ask Jesus with humility and gratitude, knowing that while sometimes He doesn't heal people here on earth, He promises forever healing for all who choose Him as the one and only Savior of their sins. There will be no more sickness or injury or need for healing in heaven (Revelation 21:4). Pray for healing not just for yourself but for anyone you know in need. And especially, pray not just for physical healing but for spiritual healing—salvation from their sins through trust in Jesus Christ as the one and only Savior.

DEAR JESUS, I KNOW YOU STILL DO MIRACLES, AND I ASK FOR HEALING FOR THIS: ____________. MOST OF ALL, YOUR WILL BE DONE. THANK YOU FOR THE HOPE OF HEAVEN, WHERE THERE WILL BE NO MORE SICKNESS, PAIN, OR INJURY. AMEN.

Don't Be Like the Wicked

Don't worry about the wicked or envy those who do wrong. For like grass, they soon fade away. Like spring flowers, they soon wither. Trust in the Lord *and do good. Then you will live safely in the land and prosper. Take delight in the* Lord, *and he will give you your heart's desires.*

Psalm 37:1–4 NLT

It seems like those who are wicked and do wrong are everywhere we turn. And sometimes it seems like no big deal to be like them and just go along with whatever seems popular, even if we know deep down that what is popular is wrong. It takes mental strength and courage not to cave to the peer pressure and join in the bad activities, especially if we're feeling the pressure from people we thought were good friends. But God promises that if we trust Him and do good, we will have everything we need, and He will give us the things that make us truly happy—because first we're happy in Him!

DEAR JESUS, PLEASE HELP ME TO STAND STRONG TO DO WHAT IS RIGHT AND GOOD ACCORDING TO YOUR WORD, EVEN UNDER PEER PRESSURE TO DO WHAT IS WICKED AND WRONG. I WANT TO DO WHAT MAKES YOU HAPPY. I TRUST THAT'S THE BEST WAY FOR ME TO BE TRULY HAPPY TOO. AMEN.

Don't Be Whiny

God is working in you, giving you the desire and the power to do what pleases him. Do everything without complaining and arguing, so that no one can criticize you. Live clean, innocent lives as children of God, shining like bright lights in a world full of crooked and perverse people.

PHILIPPIANS 2:13–15 NLT

Sometimes instead of taking good mental care of ourselves we just get whiny and grumpy about a situation we don't like. But we're far better off when we decide not to whine and complain. If you choose to be happy and grateful in every situation where you're tempted to whine and complain, think of how different your mindset might be. Think of how much more joy and peace you could have. Think of how inspiring and contagious that joy and peace could be to others. Then you can share the reasons for that joy and peace—salvation and life with Jesus Christ as Lord!

DEAR LORD, THANK YOU FOR WORKING IN ME AND GIVING ME THE POWER TO DO WHAT MAKES YOU HAPPY. HELP ME NOT TO WHINE AND COMPLAIN AND ARGUE IN ANY SITUATION BUT INSTEAD TO HAVE JOY AND GRATITUDE BECAUSE OF ALL MY BLESSINGS, ESPECIALLY THE BLESSING OF JESUS AS MY SAVIOR. AMEN.

Pep Yourself Up

"Be strong and very courageous. Be careful to obey all the law my servant Moses gave you; do not turn from it to the right or to the left, that you may be successful wherever you go. Keep this Book of the Law always on your lips; meditate on it day and night, so that you may be careful to do everything written in it. Then you will be prosperous and successful. Have I not commanded you? Be strong and courageous. Do not be afraid; do not be discouraged, for the LORD your God will be with you wherever you go."

JOSHUA 1:7–9 NIV

Do you ever give yourself a good pep talk for self-care? God gave Joshua an awesome one that we can learn from. God had called Joshua to be the one who would lead His people into the Promised Land after wandering in the desert for forty years. In Joshua 1, you can read the powerful pep talk God gave Joshua to help him be the brave new leader. It's not just for Joshua, though. You can read this scripture and let God encourage and motivate you as well, as He leads you into the wonderful plans He has for your life!

DEAR GOD, THANK YOU THAT I CAN BE STRENGTHENED AND ENCOURAGED BY THE SAME PEP TALK YOU GAVE JOSHUA. HELP ME TO REMEMBER YOUR GOOD WORDS. AMEN.

You Gotta Grow Up—But Stay Childlike Too, Part 1

When Jesus saw this, he was indignant. He said to them, "Let the little children come to me, and do not hinder them, for the kingdom of God belongs to such as these. Truly I tell you, anyone who will not receive the kingdom of God like a little child will never enter it." And he took the children in his arms, placed his hands on them and blessed them.

MARK 10:14–16 NIV

As you're going through your teen years and looking ahead to being a full-grown adult, it's exciting to think of all your goals and plans. But it's also fun to hold on to childlike youth in some ways, even while it's good (and necessary) to grow and mature. Jesus taught about a way we should always be childlike—in the way we have relationship with Him. When we're young, we're pretty carefree and eager and enthusiastic. We have great love for and faith in our parents or the ones who take care of us. And in that same kind of way, Jesus wants us to remain like children forever—by trusting in Him completely to provide for every single one of our needs and enthusiastically enjoying His great love for us.

DEAR JESUS, EVEN AS I'M GROWING UP INTO ADULTHOOD AND MATURING, HELP ME ALWAYS TO HAVE CHILDLIKE, ENTHUSIASTIC LOVE AND JOY AND FAITH IN YOU. AMEN.

You Gotta Grow Up—but Stay Childlike Too, Part 2

His disciples came and asked him, "Why do you use parables when you talk to the people?"
MATTHEW 13:10 NLT

As a little kid, you probably loved to learn from stories, and that's another way we should never lose our childlikeness. We should want to learn from the stories Jesus used in His teaching. He answered the question in Matthew 13:10 like this:

> *"This is why I speak to them in picture-stories. They have eyes but they do not see. They have ears but they do not hear and they do not understand. It happened in their lives as Isaiah said it would happen. He said, 'You hear and hear but do not understand. You look and look but do not see. . . . They hear very little with their ears. They have closed their eyes. If they did not do this, they would see with their eyes and hear with their ears and understand with their hearts. Then they would be changed in their ways, and I would heal them.'" (Matthew 13:13–15 NLV)*

Don't forget this answer from Jesus, and be praying for understanding as you study His parables and His example and all the writings in the whole Bible. We should want to have eyes and ears and minds and hearts that are open and paying attention to how God is trying to teach, guide, and love us.

LEAD ME AND HELP ME TO LEARN FROM YOU. AMEN.

You Need to Cry, Part 1

Jesus started crying.
JOHN 11:35 CEV

Crying is a necessary release of emotions, and we all need to cry sometimes as we take good care of ourselves. Jesus cried, so of course you should too! Maybe you need to cry because of frustration and sadness. Maybe you just need time and space to feel your emotions and pray about them. If you try to ignore emotions and bottle them up, they might explode in other ways or make you feel sick inside. So don't ever think crying means you're just weak or childish. Listening to and figuring out where your emotions are coming from and giving them time and space to release actually takes a lot of maturity and strength. When you can identify your emotions and realize the source of them, they don't have to overwhelm you or make you act out in unhealthy ways. Even through your tears, telling Jesus all about your emotions is one of the very best ways to deal with the hard things of life and take good care of yourself.

DEAR JESUS, PLEASE HELP ME RELEASE MY TEARS TO YOU. THANK YOU FOR LISTENING TO MY CRIES AND CARING SO MUCH ABOUT ME. HELP ME TO UNDERSTAND MY EMOTIONS AND FIGURE OUT HOW TO HANDLE THEM IN HEALTHY WAYS. AMEN.

You Need to Cry, Part 2

You, O Lord, are a covering around me, my shining-greatness, and the One Who lifts my head. I was crying to the Lord with my voice. And He answered me from His holy mountain. I lay down and slept, and I woke up again, for the Lord keeps me safe.

Psalm 3:3–5 NLV

When you just need to go to your bed or to the shower and cry your eyes out, do it! It's okay! Life can be crazy, and sometimes everything feels way too hard. As you cry and release all that emotion, think of God like your favorite blanket comforting you, for this scripture says He is the covering around you. He is the one who helps you and gives you "shining-greatness" again. He lifts your head and wants to help you get out of bed and face all the hard things head-on with His power. Remember that it's good to cry to God and tell Him all your feelings, but then always let Him lift your head again and help you keep on going.

DEAR LORD, I'M SO GRATEFUL YOU COMFORT LIKE A GENTLE COVER WHEN I'M CRYING TO YOU. AND THEN YOU LIFT MY HEAD AND GIVE ME HOPE AGAIN. THANK YOU! AMEN.

When You Want to Quit

Christ gives me the strength to face anything.
PHILIPPIANS 4:13 CEV

Just quitting seems like it would be good self-care sometimes, doesn't it? Maybe you've wished you could drop out of a class at school because it felt way too hard. Or maybe you tried a new sport but didn't want to finish the season. We've all been there. But when we do finish a semester or a season without quitting, sometimes we can look back and see how God was giving us just the right amount of courage and strength and blessing to take things one day at a time. And we can hopefully see how He used that time to grow us into better, stronger people because we endured instead of giving up. In any hard situation, you call on God to help and then trust in and wait on Him. He will either help you walk through it day by day until it's over or help you find a wise way out immediately.

FATHER GOD, PLEASE HELP ME WHEN I WANT TO IMMEDIATELY QUIT A HARD SITUATION. PLEASE BLESS ME WITH ENDURANCE, COURAGE, AND WISDOM TO KNOW WHEN TO KEEP GOING IF I NEED TO. AMEN.

You Need Peace, Not Drama

[Jesus said,] God blesses those people who make peace.
MATTHEW 5:9 CEV

You need peace, not drama, for good self-care. Isn't it frustrating how some people seem to love drama and love to stir it up for any reason? That's not something good to love. We shouldn't enjoy being in conflict with others. Instead, we should always want good and peaceable relationships—encouraging one another, forgiving one another, and not gossiping or causing fights. Jesus said God blesses those who make peace, and you can't *make* anything without some work. It takes some working out of disagreements and trouble to make peace sometimes, not just going along with anything to try to keep everyone happy and drama-free. We need wisdom to know how to do this right. Fortunately, the Bible promises us that God loves to give us wisdom (see James 1:5). Jesus wants to help us with our problems—we just have to keep on asking and listening to Him!

JESUS, PLEASE HELP ME TO MAKE PEACE, NOT DRAMA, IN MY CIRCUMSTANCES AND IN MY RELATIONSHIPS WITH OTHER PEOPLE. AMEN.

Give Your Way Over to the Lord

Be happy in the Lord. And He will give you the desires of your heart. Give your way over to the Lord. Trust in Him also. And He will do it. He will make your being right and good show as the light, and your wise actions as the noon day. Rest in the Lord and be willing to wait for Him.

PSALM 37:4–7 NLV

What does it mean to "give your way over to the Lord"? It means you say, "I don't want my own way. I want Your way instead, Lord. Guide me on the good and right paths that You have planned for me." Ask God to help you to rest in Him and let your joy come from trusting Him. He gave you your life, and you can let Him lead it. He wants to bless you in the best kind of ways both now and forever. Jesus set the greatest example of giving up His human will in order to do God the Father's will so that His work on the cross could offer salvation to all people. You can read about it in Matthew 26.

DEAR LORD, HELP ME TO WANT YOUR WAY IN MY LIFE, NOT MY OWN WAY. I WANT ALL MY HAPPINESS AND JOY TO COME FROM FOLLOWING YOU, RESTING IN YOU, AND WAITING ON YOU! AMEN.

Keep Standing Firm

Therefore, my dear brothers and sisters, stand firm. Let nothing move you. Always give yourselves fully to the work of the Lord.
1 CORINTHIANS 15:58 NIV

Being a wishy-washy person will give you a wishy-washy life. God doesn't want that for you. He wants you to stand firm in faith and following Jesus, like the apostle Paul described in this scripture. We aren't supposed to let anything move us. We need to evaluate regularly whether we have stuff going on in our lives that keeps us from standing firm and tempts us to move away from God. Have you any bad habits or activities that aren't honoring to God that you need to ditch? Are you holding on to any sins? Are you giving yourself fully to God and the good works He has planned for you? That's how you keep yourself standing firm and steady in your faith.

DEAR LORD, I WANT TO STAND STRONG AND FIRM IN MY FAITH IN YOU AND IN MY WILLINGNESS TO DO WHATEVER WORK YOU ASK OF ME. PLEASE HELP ME TO GET RID OF ANYTHING IN MY LIFE THAT WEAKENS MY RELATIONSHIP WITH YOU. AMEN.

Dealing with Enemies

"I say, love your enemies! Pray for those who persecute you! In that way, you will be acting as true children of your Father in heaven. For he gives his sunlight to both the evil and the good, and he sends rain on the just and the unjust alike. If you love only those who love you, what reward is there for that?"

MATTHEW 5:44–46 NLT

Don't battle with enemies in your mind by constantly thinking negative thoughts about them. It's just not good for you! As hard as it is to actually do, Jesus taught us that we should love and pray for our enemies. He will help us with this challenge, and when we choose to love and pray for our enemies as He taught, then, He says, we are acting like true children of God.

JESUS, IT'S REALLY HARD TO LOVE AND PRAY FOR THE PEOPLE WHO TREAT ME TERRIBLY! BUT I WANT TO DO MY BEST AT THIS WITH YOUR HELP BECAUSE I LOVE YOU AND WANT TO OBEY YOU. IT'S ONLY WITH YOUR POWER THAT I CAN CHOOSE TO DO THIS. I'M TRUSTING YOU TO HELP ME, AND I PRAY FOR THESE PEOPLE WHO FEEL LIKE ENEMIES RIGHT NOW. . .

Remind Yourself of God's Unstoppable, Amazing Love

Can anything ever separate us from Christ's love? Does it mean he no longer loves us if we have trouble or calamity, or are persecuted, or hungry, or destitute, or in danger, or threatened with death? . . . No, despite all these things, overwhelming victory is ours through Christ, who loved us. And I am convinced that nothing can ever separate us from God's love. Neither death nor life, neither angels nor demons, neither our fears for today nor our worries about tomorrow—not even the powers of hell can separate us from God's love. No power in the sky above or in the earth below—indeed, nothing in all creation will ever be able to separate us from the love of God that is revealed in Christ Jesus our Lord.

ROMANS 8:35, 37–39 NLT

The Bible promises that even the strongest forces, the most extreme circumstances, and the very worst things of this world can't keep away God's superpowerful love for us through Jesus. Your self-care routines should regularly include reminding yourself of how awesome this truth is!

JESUS, THANK YOU THAT ABSOLUTELY NOTHING CAN STOP YOUR AWESOME LOVE FOR ME OR KEEP ME AWAY FROM IT. AMEN.

Don't Live in Fear

[Jesus said:] "Don't be afraid of those who threaten you. For the time is coming when everything that is covered will be revealed, and all that is secret will be made known to all. . . . Don't be afraid of those who want to kill your body; they cannot touch your soul. Fear only God, who can destroy both soul and body in hell."
MATTHEW 10:26, 28 NLT

It's not healthy to live in fear, so don't let yourself do it! Jesus taught us that we don't have anything to fear. Evil people and evil plans will be uncovered—if not right away, then eventually. Above all, God sees and cares and will bring consequences and justice. We can constantly pray for Him to do that and for wisdom about how to be strong against enemies—and for protection and courage too!

DEAR LORD, REMIND ME EVERY DAY THAT I DON'T NEED TO BE AFRAID OF ANYONE. YOU SEE AND KNOW EVERYTHING, AND YOU PROTECT AND PROVIDE FOR ME. YOU WILL MAKE EVERYTHING RIGHT IN YOUR PERFECT TIMING. YOU ARE THE ONLY ONE I SHOULD FEAR, AND THAT MEANS I SHOULD RESPECT YOU. YOU ARE MY SAVIOR, AND I KNOW HOW MUCH YOU LOVE ME. AMEN.

Embrace Your Weirdness

Dear friends, your real home is not here on earth.
You are strangers here. I ask you to keep away from all the sinful
desires of the flesh. These things fight to get hold of your soul.
1 PETER 2:11 NLV

It's weird to be a true Christian in this world—and that's a good thing, because God's Word tells us to expect it. So just embrace the weirdness. Be content with it, and don't let it make you lose any self-confidence. Some versions of 1 Peter 2:11 describe Christians as being like aliens on earth in the sense that we are strangers here because this world is not our real home. When we choose Jesus as Savior, we know that He will give us eternal life someday in heaven, which *is* our real home. So, we should be careful not to follow what the world says is right if it goes against what God says is right. Being a true Christian isn't always easy, but it is always totally worth it!

DEAR LORD, NO MATTER HOW WEIRD I FEEL BECAUSE OF IT, HELP ME TO FOLLOW YOUR WAYS AND WISDOM MORE THAN ANYTHING ELSE IN THIS WORLD—BECAUSE I KNOW MY REAL HOME IS IN HEAVEN WITH YOU. GIVE ME SOLID SELF-CONFIDENCE THAT COMES FROM TRUSTING IN YOU AS MY ULTIMATE CONFIDENCE. AMEN.

The Incredible Greatness of God's Power

I pray that your hearts will be flooded with light so that you can understand the confident hope he has given to those he called—his holy people who are his rich and glorious inheritance. I also pray that you will understand the incredible greatness of God's power for us who believe him. This is the same mighty power that raised Christ from the dead and seated him in the place of honor at God's right hand in the heavenly realms.

EPHESIANS 1:18–20 NLT

In this scripture passage, the apostle Paul was sharing his prayers with the Christians who lived in Ephesus. Those same prayers are what God wants for you as a Christian today too. If you believe in Jesus as your only Savior, you belong to Him and you have hope for the awesome things God has planned for you. And His power for you is so great—it is the same power that brought Jesus back to life! That supernatural power is working in you now so you can do the good things God wants for you, and it will be working in you forever because it has given you eternal life.

DEAR LORD, HELP ME TO SEE AND BELIEVE MORE EVERY DAY ABOUT HOW GREAT YOU ARE, HOW AWESOME YOUR POWER IS, HOW MUCH YOU LOVE ME. AMEN.

Quiet Time and Space to Pray

Very early the next morning before daylight, Jesus got up and went to a place where he could be alone and pray. Simon and the others started looking for him. And when they found him, they said, "Everyone is looking for you!"

MARK 1:35–37 CEV

Jesus had many things to do and many people wanting to see Him, hear Him, learn from Him, and be healed by Him. But even with all this going on, He took time to get away and pray. We need to learn from Him how important it is to take quiet time and space to pray. If even Jesus who was sinless and perfect needed alone time to rest away from other people and to spend time in prayer, how much more do we need that kind of time?

DEAR JESUS, REMIND ME REGULARLY OF YOUR EXAMPLE OF QUIET TIME AND SPACE TO PRAY. I DON'T WANT OTHER RESPONSIBILITIES TO GET IN THE WAY OF PUTTING YOU FIRST IN MY LIFE. PLEASE HELP ME TO BALANCE MY SCHEDULE AND RESPONSIBILITIES WELL. AMEN.

Remember You Have Life to the Full

[Jesus said,] "I am the gate; whoever enters through me will be saved. They will come in and go out, and find pasture. The thief comes only to steal and kill and destroy; I have come that they may have life, and have it to the full."

JOHN 10:9–10 NIV

The devil is a thief and a killer and a destroyer. But no matter what he tries to do to us, he cannot win. We will ultimately prevail against him in the end because of Jesus. The devil might hurt us or make us stumble away from Jesus at times, but he will never totally defeat us if Jesus is our Savior. Jesus gives life to the full, and no one can ever, ever take that away. Remind yourself every day of this truth!

FATHER, THANK YOU SO MUCH THAT NOTHING CAN EVER TAKE AWAY YOUR MOST VALUABLE GIFT TO ME—ETERNAL LIFE—BECAUSE YOU CHOSE ME AS YOUR CHILD. AMEN.

You Always Need Reminders

The Holy Spirit will come and help you, because the Father will send the Spirit to take my place. The Spirit will teach you everything and will remind you of what I said while I was with you. I give you peace, the kind of peace only I can give. It isn't like the peace this world can give. So don't be worried or afraid.

John 14:26–27 CEV

Do you ever take care of yourself with sticky note reminders of what you need to do? Or texts or emails to yourself? We're all forgetful sometimes, and Jesus understands that. He taught that the Holy Spirit would come both to teach us and to remind us of all the things He said. He knows we need constant encouragement and reminders of truth. Think of how hard it would be to keep on track with God's Word in our culture today if we didn't have the Spirit constantly encouraging us to remember it!

DEAR LORD, I'M GRATEFUL FOR THE HOLY SPIRIT
TEACHING ME AND REMINDING ME OF ALL THAT YOU SAID.
IT'S GOOD TO HAVE YOU WITH ME ALL THE TIME. AMEN.

Accept the Facts of Tests and Trials

God blesses those who patiently endure testing and temptation. Afterward they will receive the crown of life that God has promised to those who love him. And remember, when you are being tempted, do not say, "God is tempting me." God is never tempted to do wrong, and he never tempts anyone else. Temptation comes from our own desires, which entice us and drag us away. These desires give birth to sinful actions. And when sin is allowed to grow, it gives birth to death.

JAMES 1:12–15 NLT

God's Word is clear that we will be tested and go through many trials. Even though that's true, it's still the best kind of life to love God and trust in and follow Jesus as Lord and Savior. In every test and trial, every bit of suffering and heartache, God is working out His good plans in our lives when we faithfully obey Him no matter our circumstances. He blesses us with His supernatural comfort, peace, and joy even in the midst of trials and pain, until one day we will have total comfort, peace, and joy—and no tears or hardship ever again—when we are at home forever in heaven.

DEAR LORD, HELP ME TO ACCEPT TESTS AND TRIALS, AND PLEASE HELP ME TO PATIENTLY ENDURE THEM AND LEARN FROM THEM. I WANT TO OVERCOME THEM BECAUSE I FOLLOW YOU AND HAVE FAITH IN YOUR FOREVER BLESSINGS.

Choose the Right Influencer

So don't boast about following a particular human leader. For everything belongs to you—whether Paul or Apollos or Peter, or the world, or life and death, or the present and the future. Everything belongs to you, and you belong to Christ, and Christ belongs to God.

1 CORINTHIANS 3:21–23 NLT

Do you have influencers you watch to teach you about self-care? You might be impressed by and look up to certain celebrities and influencers, but be sure to choose Jesus as your number one influencer—far above and beyond all others. God the Father sent His Son, Jesus Christ, to earth to be a human being just like us and to be our example for living the best kind of life. And how do we keep following His example? By reading and studying God's Word to keep learning more and more about who God is and how Jesus lived. And by keeping in close relationship with Jesus through prayer and worship.

JESUS, YOU ARE MY VERY BEST INFLUENCER AND ROLE MODEL. PLEASE HELP ME TO LOVE LEARNING ABOUT YOU AND TO KEEP GROWING CLOSER TO YOU. GIVE ME WISDOM ABOUT OTHER INFLUENCES IN MY LIFE, AND HELP ME TO STOP FOLLOWING ANYONE WHO IS NOT GOOD FOR ME AND MY RELATIONSHIP WITH YOU. AMEN.

Get and Give God's Comfort

God is our merciful Father and the source of all comfort. He comforts us in all our troubles so that we can comfort others. When they are troubled, we will be able to give them the same comfort God has given us. For the more we suffer for Christ, the more God will shower us with his comfort through Christ. Even when we are weighed down with troubles, it is for your comfort and salvation!
2 CORINTHIANS 1:3–6 NLT

Imagine a totally trouble-free life. We wouldn't have much need for self-care if we never had any troubles! What a dream world that would be—but it won't happen until heaven because hard times and troubles are unavoidable in this life. But when we go through them, we have the awesome promise that God will comfort us. Not only that, but there is purpose in our troubles and our comfort because we can use our experiences to comfort and help others. That can even lead more people to salvation in Jesus Christ. Think back to ways you have felt God's comfort or are feeling it right now. Then praise God and make plans for how you can help share comfort with others.

DEAR LORD, I THANK YOU FOR ALL THE WAYS YOU COMFORT AND BRING ME PEACE, EVEN IN THE WORST OF TROUBLES. HELP ME TO FEEL AND REMEMBER THAT COMFORT WELL AND PASS IT ALONG TO OTHERS WHILE SHARING WITH THEM ABOUT YOUR LOVE AND SALVATION. AMEN.

Keep Your Mind Clean and Clear

For a time is coming when people will no longer listen to sound and wholesome teaching. They will follow their own desires and will look for teachers who will tell them whatever their itching ears want to hear. They will reject the truth and chase after myths. But you should keep a clear mind in every situation.

2 TIMOTHY 4:3–5 NLT

You have the choice to take good care of your mind by filling it with what is true and right and pure and noble and excellent and worthy of praise (Philippians 4:8)—or what is sinful and evil and scary and wrong according to Gods' Word. There's a lot of good stuff in movies, shows, books, music, magazines, and endless websites and social media. But there's a lot of really awful stuff too. And we make it harder and harder to listen to Jesus if we fill our minds with too much media. That's why in such a confusing world with so much evil and so many false teachers, it's more important than ever to be extra, *extra* careful about what we watch, read, and listen to (and how much) and what activities we participate in. Jesus is always near through His Holy Spirit, but how much do we tune Him out by the junk we jam into our brains?

JESUS, HELP ME EMPTY MY MIND OF THE THINGS THAT AREN'T GOOD FOR ME. I WANT TO KEEP MY MIND CLEAR SO THAT I CAN EASILY HEAR THE BEST THINGS FROM YOU. AMEN.

Care Like Jesus

Jesus cured many people of their diseases, illnesses, and evil spirits, and he restored sight to many who were blind. Then he told John's disciples, "Go back to John and tell him what you have seen and heard—the blind see, the lame walk, those with leprosy are cured, the deaf hear, the dead are raised to life, and the Good News is being preached to the poor."

LUKE 7:21–22 NLT

Jesus loved and cared for people like no other human ever has or ever will. He healed and provided for the sick and needy. He reached out to the lonely and unwanted. He boldly taught the truth and showed people the one and only way to God in heaven. And if we are true followers of Jesus, then we will do our best at these things too! Keep asking Jesus how He wants you to be like Him, care for the needs of others, and help spread His truth.

JESUS, LIKE YOU, I WANT TO LOVE AND REACH OUT TO AND CARE FOR PEOPLE. PLEASE HELP ME. AMEN.

Pray Persistently

Jesus told his disciples a story about how they should keep on praying and never give up: In a town there was once a judge who didn't fear God or care about people. In that same town there was a widow who kept going to the judge and saying, "Make sure that I get fair treatment in court." For a while the judge refused to do anything. Finally, he said to himself, "Even though I don't fear God or care about people, I will help this widow because she keeps on bothering me. If I don't help her, she will wear me out." The Lord said: Think about what that crooked judge said. Won't God protect his chosen ones who pray to him day and night? Won't he be concerned for them? He will surely hurry and help them.

LUKE 18:1–8 CEV

Good self-care is not just a onetime thing, and neither is prayer! Jesus gave us this example in Luke 18 to teach us to pray continuously with persistence—don't stop! The point is that if a judge in the courts who did not even respect God was finally willing to help the woman who kept asking and asking, how much more will God help His people who keep asking for His help?

JESUS, I'M SO VERY THANKFUL THAT YOU NEVER GET TIRED OF MY PRAYERS. AMEN.

Give with Great Faith

A poor woman whose husband had died came by and gave two very small pieces of money.
MARK 12:42 NLV

One day Jesus watched many rich people give large offerings to God at the temple. Giving a lot wasn't hard for them because they were so rich that they had plenty of money to share. But then Jesus watched a very poor widow drop in two coins that were worth less than one cent. And Jesus said to His disciples, "This poor widow has given more money than all the others." But how was that possible? Jesus said, "The rich people put in money they didn't even need because they have so much extra. But the poor widow had nothing extra. She needed every bit of her money to live on, but still she gave it all to God."

JESUS, I WANT TO GIVE TO YOU WITH GREAT FAITH JUST LIKE THIS WIDOW DID, BECAUSE I TRUST THAT YOU WILL PROVIDE FOR ME NO MATTER WHAT, AND YOUR BLESSINGS ARE GREATER THAN ANYTHING I COULD EVER GAIN ON MY OWN. AMEN.

Journal for Self-Care, Part 1

Let us keep running in the race that God has planned for us. Let us keep looking to Jesus. Our faith comes from Him and He is the One Who makes it perfect. He did not give up when He had to suffer shame and die on a cross. He knew of the joy that would be His later. Now He is sitting at the right side of God.
HEBREWS 12:1–2 NLV

Jesus was able to endure suffering on the cross because of the joy that He was looking forward to later. And if we've asked Jesus to be our Savior, then we also have unspeakable joy waiting for us in heaven. There's lots of joy along the way here on earth too, even in the midst of suffering and sorrow we might experience. Do you like to do journaling? Can you journal about your joys? It's a great idea to keep track of all the joys and blessings, big and small, that God gives us to help encourage us to keep going and not give up along the race of life He has mapped out for us.

DEAR JESUS, I'LL KEEP LOOKING TO YOU AND WRITING DOWN AND REMEMBERING. THANK YOU FOR THE JOYS I HAVE NOW AND THE FOREVER JOY THAT'S AHEAD! AMEN.

Journal for Self-Care, Part 2

I passed on to you what was most important and what had also been passed on to me. Christ died for our sins, just as the Scriptures said. He was buried, and he was raised from the dead on the third day, just as the Scriptures said. He was seen by Peter and then by the Twelve. After that, he was seen by more than 500 of his followers at one time, most of whom are still alive, though some have died. Then he was seen by James and later by all the apostles. Last of all, as though I had been born at the wrong time, I also saw him.

1 CORINTHIANS 15:3–8 NLT

Like the apostle Paul did, it's good to write down and remember the main reasons for our faith and hope in Jesus Christ. The gospel message and the proof with eyewitnesses of our risen Savior is the best news we can ever know and share! So keep jotting things down in a journal that keep you encouraged to stand strong in your faith in Jesus!

JESUS, YOU ARE ALIVE, AND I PRAISE YOU! I DON'T EVER WANT TO FORGET OR STOP BEING EXCITED ABOUT HOW AWESOME THE MESSAGE OF THE GOSPEL IS. WHAT YOU DID TO SAVE ALL PEOPLE WHO CHOOSE TO REPENT FROM SIN AND BELIEVE IN YOU IS ASTOUNDING! HELP ME NEVER TO FORGET IT AND NEVER STOP SHARING IT WITH OTHERS. AMEN.

Self-Care When You've Lost Someone You Love

We want you to know for sure about those who have died. You have no reason to have sorrow as those who have no hope. We believe that Jesus died and then came to life again. Because we believe this, we know that God will bring to life again all those who belong to Jesus.

1 THESSALONIANS 4:13–14 NLV

When someone we love dies, we experience sadness and pain, and we miss that person like crazy. But for all who trust in Jesus as Savior, this life on earth is not all there is. If you know that the loved one you've lost trusted Jesus as Savior, then you can be confident that they are in heaven with God. And with Jesus as your Savior, God is with you through the Holy Spirit. So God is with your loved one, and God is with you. In a way, you are not that far apart at all! It's still so sad and hard not to talk with or hug or share life with your loved one who has died, though, of course—but we have new life and perfect heaven to look forward to, where we will spend forever with Jesus and all of our loved ones who chose Him too. If you have loved ones who have not yet chosen to trust in Jeus, keep praying for them to do so!

DEAR JESUS, PLEASE COMFORT ME AND HELP ME TO TAKE GOOD CARE WHEN I HAVE LOST SOMEONE I LOVE. THANK YOU THAT I DON'T HAVE TO GRIEVE WITHOUT HOPE. AMEN.

What to Do When Someone Sins Against You

"If another believer sins against you, go privately and point out the offense. If the other person listens and confesses it, you have won that person back."
MATTHEW 18:15 NLT

Jesus taught about how to deal with conflict with fellow believers in the right ways. If someone has sinned against us, hurt us, or upset us, sometimes we will need to have hard conversations to work things out and help improve the relationship and situation. It can be so difficult to do, but it's not right to talk about the offending person to others behind his or her back. Jesus taught us to go to that person one-on-one. We should pray for Jesus to give us peace and wisdom and to help us communicate well and resolve the conflict constructively as we let Him help us.

JESUS, PLEASE HELP ME TO CHOOSE TO OBEY YOU WHEN SOMEONE SINS AGAINST ME. I WANT TO HANDLE CONFLICT THE RIGHT WAY—YOUR WAY. AMEN.

Deal with Demons?

When Jesus stepped ashore, he was met by a demon-possessed man from the town. For a long time this man had not worn clothes or lived in a house, but had lived in the tombs. When he saw Jesus, he cried out and fell at his feet, shouting at the top of his voice, "What do you want with me, Jesus, Son of the Most High God? I beg you, don't torture me!" For Jesus had commanded the impure spirit to come out of the man. Many times it had seized him, and though he was chained hand and foot and kept under guard, he had broken his chains and had been driven by the demon into solitary places.

LUKE 8:27–29 NIV

The world might tell you to "deal with your demons" for self-care. You can find all kinds of strange and scary information if you go looking for it. But go to God's Word for the truth about demonic forces. While it can be frightening to think of demons, we can remember that Jesus has all power over them. In Luke 8, He sent the demons out of a man and into a herd of pigs! Jesus can do anything to protect and rescue those who have faith in Him!

JESUS, WHEN I FEEL AFRAID, REMIND ME OF YOUR POWER AGAINST ANY EVIL FORCE. PLEASE GIVE ME COURAGE. KEEP ME CLOSE AND PROTECT ME, I PRAY. AMEN.

Fresh Each Morning

Yet I still dare to hope when I remember this: The faithful love of the Lord never ends! His mercies never cease. Great is his faithfulness; his mercies begin afresh each morning. I say to myself, "The Lord is my inheritance; therefore, I will hope in him!" The Lord is good to those who depend on him, to those who search for him.

Lamentations 3:21–25 NLT

When you wake up on a new day, how do you feel? Hopefully you've gotten some good sleep and you feel like you have a fresh start no matter what happened yesterday. God's Word talks about how your heavenly Father's love and mercy are new to you every morning. As you open your eyes and get out of bed, before you start any morning self-care routine, think of this scripture in Lamentations and let it inspire you to head into your day with God's awesome joy and peace filling you up—and then share it with those around you.

DEAR LORD, THANK YOU FOR BRAND-NEW DAYS WITH FRESH STARTS. I TRUST IN YOU AND YOUR POWER AND GOODNESS TO ME—TODAY AND EVERY DAY. AMEN.

Mary Knew About the Best Self-Care

Martha welcomed him into her house. And she had a sister called Mary, who sat at the Lord's feet and listened to his teaching.
LUKE 10:38–39 ESV

Jesus was coming over! Mary and Martha, two sisters who loved Jesus, were excited to welcome Him into their home. Martha was gifted at planning and preparing and overseeing all the important details, and she probably wanted everything to be perfect for such an important guest. But Martha got really upset with Mary because when Jesus arrived, Mary didn't help her with all the work of hosting and serving. Mary instead sat at Jesus' feet to listen to everything He had to say. Both sisters loved Jesus and were showing it in their own unique ways. But Jesus lovingly told Martha that Mary had made the better choice by simply enjoying His company and listening to His teaching. Mary gives us an example that the best kind of self-care is to rest in and learn from Jesus!

DEAR JESUS, I WANT TO REST IN AND LEARN FROM YOU SO MUCH MORE THAN RUSHING AROUND TRYING TO GET ALL THE DETAILS OF LIFE RIGHT. PLEASE HELP ME TO CRAVE TIME IN YOUR PRESENCE. AMEN.

Salty and Shiny

"You are the salt of the earth. But what good is salt if it has lost its flavor? . . . You are the light of the world—like a city on a hilltop that cannot be hidden. . . . In the same way, let your good deeds shine out for all to see, so that everyone will praise your heavenly Father."

MATTHEW 5:13–14, 16 NLT

Maybe you like to use a salt scrub in your self-care routines. They smell good and make your skin so soft! If you do use one, let it remind you that Jesus taught us that we should want to be like salt and light. Salt is most commonly used to help food taste its best, and we too should want to bring out the best in others and show them life at its very best. Life at its best is a life that believes in and follows Jesus. Jesus also wants us to be the light of the world. If we hide our light, we can't help others see the way to Jesus. But if we shine our light, giving Him honor through every good thing we do, we help others honor Him too.

DEAR JESUS, HELP ME TO REMEMBER WHAT YOU TAUGHT ABOUT SALT AND LIGHT. HELP ME TO BE SALTY AND SHINING! I WANT TO REACH OUT AND SHINE YOUR LOVE TO OTHERS, HELPING THEM KNOW AND LOVE YOU TOO! AMEN.

Build Wisely on Jesus

"Everyone who hears these words of mine and puts them into practice is like a wise man who built his house on the rock. The rain came down, the streams rose, and the winds blew and beat against that house; yet it did not fall, because it had its foundation on the rock. But everyone who hears these words of mine and does not put them into practice is like a foolish man who built his house on sand. The rain came down, the streams rose, and the winds blew and beat against that house, and it fell with a great crash."

MATTHEW 7:24–27 NIV

You have to build your life wisely on rock if you want to take good care of yourself. Jesus taught with a parable that compared people who hear His teaching and listen and obey it with people who only hear it but do nothing with it. Those who obey Jesus are built up strong for whatever life brings their way, while those who ignore Jesus are easily washed away. So, what are you building your life on?

DEAR JESUS, I ALWAYS WANT TO BE ABLE TO SAY I'M BUILDING ON YOU, MY ROCK! PLEASE STRENGTHEN ME WITH GREAT FAITH AS I DEPEND ON YOU TO BE MY FIRM FOUNDATION IN EVERY KIND OF WEATHER! AMEN.

Remember That God Can Make It Good

Joseph replied, "Don't be afraid of me. Am I God, that I can punish you? You intended to harm me, but God intended it all for good. He brought me to this position so I could save the lives of many people. No, don't be afraid. I will continue to take care of you and your children." So he reassured them by speaking kindly to them.

GENESIS 50:19–21 NLT

For good mental health, you need lots of reminders that God can take the very worst of situations and turn them upside down. He can take anyone's bad plans toward you and work them out for your good. Think about the story of Joseph. It doesn't get much worse than being sold by your siblings into slavery in another country! You can read the whole story of Joseph's life in Genesis 37, 39–50 and see the way God blessed Joseph because of that awful experience. Whatever you are going through today, no matter how hard it is, choose to be loyal and obedient to God like Joseph was, and in His perfect timing God will bless you for your faithfulness.

DEAR LORD, YOU CAN TAKE ANYTHING THAT'S MEANT TO BE BAD FOR ME AND TURN IT INTO GOOD. I BELIEVE THAT, AND I TRUST YOU! AMEN.

When You Need Good Energy

God saved you by his grace when you believed. And you can't take credit for this; it is a gift from God. Salvation is not a reward for the good things we have done, so none of us can boast about it. For we are God's masterpiece. He has created us anew in Christ Jesus, so we can do the good things he planned for us long ago.
EPHESIANS 2:8–10 NLT

You don't need energy drinks. They can be bad for you in the long run. So if you're ever feeling blah and tired and unmotivated about anything in life, let Ephesians 2:8–10 energize you—and keep coming back to it any time you need reenergized. When you think about how God created you on purpose with good plans for your life and how you have the gift of salvation because you committed your life to Jesus Christ, you should feel full of gratitude and enthusiasm! You should be eager to keep following Jesus. You should be asking Him to guide you in doing all those good things He has ready and scheduled for you in His perfect timing.

DEAR JESUS, AS I FOLLOW YOU, KEEP ME EXCITED AND EAGER FOR YOU TO SHOW ME ALL THE GOOD THINGS YOU WANT ME TO DO WITH MY LIFE. DAY BY DAY, I'LL TRUST YOU AS MY GUIDE AND MY BEST SOURCE OF ENERGY AND ENTHUSIASM. AMEN.

Angels Help Take Good Care of You!

[Jesus said,] "See that you do not despise one of these little ones. For I tell you that their angels in heaven always see the face of my Father in heaven."
MATTHEW 18:10 NIV

Stories and movies might try to give us some ideas about what angels do and what they look like, but real truth about angels is in the Bible. The bottom line is that they are real. Jesus said so! So, don't forget about angels, and let the fact of their existence encourage you. They help take good care of you! Study the Bible to truly learn about them. Ask Jesus to send His help and care and protection through them. Let these scriptures teach and encourage you:

> *The angel of the Lord stays close around those who fear Him, and He takes them out of trouble. (Psalm 34:7 NLV)*
>
> *Keep on loving one another as brothers and sisters. Do not forget to show hospitality to strangers, for by so doing some people have shown hospitality to angels without knowing it. (Hebrews 13:1–2 NIV)*

DEAR JESUS, I'M GRATEFUL TO KNOW THAT ANGELS HELPING WATCH OUT FOR AND TAKE CARE OF ME ISN'T JUST A MYTH OR FAIRY TALE. HELP ME TO LEARN MORE TRUTH ABOUT THEM FROM YOUR WORD. THANK YOU FOR YOUR PROTECTION AND LOVE! AMEN.

She Was Immediately Healed!

A woman in the crowd had suffered for twelve years with constant bleeding, and she could find no cure. Coming up behind Jesus, she touched the fringe of his robe. Immediately, the bleeding stopped. "Who touched me?" Jesus asked. . . . "Someone deliberately touched me, for I felt healing power go out from me." When the woman realized that she could not stay hidden, she began to tremble and fell to her knees in front of him. The whole crowd heard her explain why she had touched him and that she had been immediately healed. "Daughter," he said to her, "your faith has made you well. Go in peace."

LUKE 8:43–48 NLT

If you've ever had a cold that just never seemed to end, you know how sick of being sick you get, even for a matter of days or weeks. The poor bleeding woman in the Bible had been sick for twelve years! Can you imagine how awful that would have been? But she had heard of Jesus, and she had great faith in His power. She was sure that if she just touched the bottom of His cloak, she would be healed. So she did, and she was!

DEAR JESUS, HELP ME TO HAVE SUCH AWESOME FAITH IN YOUR POWER TO HEAL. AMEN.

The Spirit Is Willing, But. . .

[Jesus said:] "Keep watch and pray, so that you will not give in to temptation. For the spirit is willing, but the body is weak!"
MATTHEW 26:41 NLT

Sometimes we have good intentions to care for ourselves well with a good schedule and good priority list. But then we just don't follow through. Can you relate? Do you ever plan to study really well with good time management for an upcoming test but then find yourself quickly cramming the night before? Do you plan to have regular quiet time with Jesus, but you keep letting everything else in your life take priority over Him?

We are human, and we have struggles and temptations that keep us from doing the good things that we should do and that we intend to do. That's why we need to pray for help. We need to tell Jesus, "I can't do this on my own! Because of sin, I'm tempted to mess up all the time! I need Your awesome power working in me to overcome this temptation."

DEAR JESUS, PLEASE HELP ME WITH EVERY LITTLE THING, INCLUDING PRIORITIES AND SCHEDULING AND TIME MANAGEMENT! I'M SO GLAD YOU CARE ABOUT THE DETAILS OF MY LIFE. AMEN.

Tell Yourself "Even If"

Even if an army gathers against me, my heart will not be afraid. Even if war rises against me, I will be sure of You.

Psalm 27:3 NLV

Give your mental health a boost by letting this scripture inspire you to think of all kinds of "even if " statements to affirm how you will keep on letting Jesus be your source of courage, strength, love, and salvation!

"Even if this test tomorrow is hard, I will trust You to help me do my best, Jesus!"

"Even if this sickness does not go away, I know You love and care for me in the middle of it, Jesus!"

"Even if you don't heal this injury here on earth like I know You can, I trust that You heal forever in heaven, Jesus!"

"Even if I make mistakes, I know You love and forgive me, Jesus!"

DEAR JESUS, I BELIEVE THAT EVEN IF EVERYTHING ELSE IN LIFE FAILS, YOU NEVER FAIL ME. EVEN IF MY PLANS FALL APART, YOURS NEVER DO. EVEN IF I THINK I CAN'T DO SOMETHING, WITH YOUR HELP, ACCORDING TO YOUR PERFECT WILL, I CAN. AND THROUGH IT ALL, YOU LOVE AND TAKE GOOD CARE OF ME. THANK YOU! AMEN.

Boast Only About the Lord

As the Scriptures say, "If you want to boast, boast only about the Lord.*"*
2 Corinthians 10:17 NLT

Be sure to celebrate the successes in your life. An awesome part of self-care is to enjoy an accomplishment, especially when it's something that has required commitment and hard work. Of course you should feel happy and excited. But we all have to be very careful that we don't forget to give our Lord Jesus credit when we're celebrating. It's a great way to stay humble and never become full of pride in ourselves. Our Lord is the one who deserves all the praise and worship because He is the one who created us and gives us all our gifts, talents, and abilities.

LORD JESUS, YOU ARE MY CREATOR! YOU ARE THE ONE WHO MAKES ME CAPABLE OF ACCOMPLISHING GREAT THINGS. I WANT TO BE SUCCESSFUL FOR YOUR PRAISE AND GLORY! PLEASE HELP ME TO USE MY GIFTS WELL IN THE WAYS YOU WANT ME TO, ESPECIALLY TO POINT OTHERS TO TRUSTING IN YOU AS SAVIOR. AMEN.

Protect Your Mind from False Prophets

[Jesus said:] Watch out for false prophets! They dress up like sheep, but inside they are wolves who have come to attack you. You can tell what they are by what they do. . . . You can tell who the false prophets are by their deeds.
MATTHEW 7:15–16, 20 CEV

We have to take good care of our mental health by protecting ourselves against false prophets and teachers. Jesus warned strongly against them for good reason. There are some really confusing differences among churches and people who call themselves Christians. Some differences are no big deal because they're just a matter of traditions and different preferences. But some differences result from churches and teachers and preachers going against the Word of God. Second Corinthians 11:13 (CEV) says these false teachers "only pretend to be apostles of Christ." Jesus is not surprised by these false teachers and churches, so we don't have to be afraid. If we keep ourselves strongly dependent on Jesus and the Bible through the Holy Spirit, He will help us figure out the false teachers and churches from the ones that truly know, love, and serve Him and that preach the *whole* Word of God.

DEAR JESUS, PLEASE HELP ME TO PROTECT MY MIND FROM FALSE PROPHETS AND TEACHERS—ANYONE TWISTING YOUR WORD AND TRYING TO DRAW ME INTO SIN AND AWAY FROM CLOSE RELATIONSHIP WITH YOU. AMEN.

In God's Hands

But I trust in you, Lord; I say, "You are my God."
My times are in your hands.
Psalm 31:14–15 NIV

As you're going through your teen years, you may feel stressed about the future and plans for after high school. Or maybe you're stressed because you can't seem to decide on any good plans. Or perhaps you're just trying not to worry and you're taking things day by day! Whatever the case, never stop talking to God and asking for His help in setting goals for your life. You are so blessed that, like the psalmist says in Psalm 31, your times are in God's hands. Ask Him for His wisdom and to open the right doors of opportunity for you—the ones that He knows are best for you to walk through, that match up with His will for your life and the good things He has planned for you to do. And ask Him to close doors that you shouldn't walk through, ones that might take you down the wrong paths. Remember that God sees and knows everything that is going on with you, and He loves you like no one else does!

DEAR GOD, I BELIEVE MY TIMES ARE IN YOUR HANDS. YOU HOLD ME, PROTECT ME, AND TAKE GOOD CARE OF ME. PLEASE LEAD ME! OPEN THE RIGHT DOORS OF OPPORTUNITIES YOU WANT FOR ME, AND CLOSE THE ONES THAT WOULD BE WRONG FOR ME. HELP ME TO SEE YOUR WILL CLEARLY. AMEN.

Keep Your Mind in Perfect Peace

You will keep in perfect peace those whose minds are steadfast, because they trust in you. Trust in the LORD forever, for the LORD, the LORD himself, is the Rock eternal. . . . The path of the righteous is level; you, the Upright One, make the way of the righteous smooth. Yes, LORD, walking in the way of your laws, we wait for you; your name and renown are the desire of our hearts. My soul yearns for you in the night; in the morning my spirit longs for you.

ISAIAH 26:3–4, 7–9 NIV

Perfect peace almost sounds way too good to be true, doesn't it? There always seems to be something stressing us out, even if it's just a family squabble or an overwhelming homework assignment. But God's Word tells us how to have perfect peace, and we need it so much for good mental health care! We can have perfect peace by trusting in God and fixing our thoughts on Him. When we feel our peace being disrupted, we need to turn our attention back to God and ask for His help to handle what's causing the stress. One simple way to do this is just to start singing to Him, even just in your mind, anytime you feel stressed out. Truly worship the Lord and be amazed as His supernatural peace fills you.

DEAR GOD, I NEED MY MIND AND BODY TO BE FILLED WITH YOUR PERFECT PEACE. PLEASE HELP ME TO TURN MY THOUGHTS BACK TO YOU IN STRESSFUL SITUATIONS—AND THEN KEEP THEM THERE! AMEN.

It's the Lord You Are Serving

Whatever you do, work at it with all your heart,
as working for the Lord, not for human masters, since you
know that you will receive an inheritance from the Lord
as a reward. It is the Lord Christ you are serving.
Colossians 3:23–24 NIV

Don't let yourself get too overwhelmed in life. All your studying, work, relationships, and responsibilities can sometimes feel like too much and too hard. So, take it all to Jesus. Tell Him how overwhelmed you feel. Maybe you need to reprioritize some things, and He can give you wisdom about that. He cares about your feelings and loves to help you. And you can do any task or assignment as if it's praise and honor to the Lord. Do your best at it no matter what it is, and say, "Jesus, I want to bring glory and honor to You with the way I work at this and with my attitude in the middle of it."

JESUS, REMIND ME THAT NO MATTER WHAT I'M DOING, I CAN DO IT IN A WAY TO HONOR YOU IF I FOCUS MY MIND ON PRAISING AND THANKING YOU IN THE MIDDLE OF IT. HELP ME TO FEEL NOT OVERWHELMED BUT FULL OF JOY INSTEAD. AMEN.

Dealing with Fear and Anxiety

I will honor the Lord at all times. His praise will always be in my mouth. My soul will be proud to tell about the Lord. Let those who suffer hear it and be filled with joy. Give great honor to the Lord with me. Let us praise His name together. I looked for the Lord, and He answered me. And He took away all my fears.

Psalm 34:1–4 NLV

Maybe you've gone through a traumatic experience that now causes you to struggle with anxiety. If you've ever lost a loved one, you might have fears of losing someone else too. If you've ever been in a bad car accident, you might struggle with a fear of driving or riding in cars. If you've ever been bitten by a dog, you might have a fear of dogs. If you've ever had a close call with tornadoes or hurricanes, you might be more scared of bad weather in the future. Unfortunately, our bad experiences in the past create some of the fears we have now. But God knows each of us individually so well. He knows all about every hard and sad and scary thing we've ever endured. He knows every detail about us, down to the very number of hairs on our heads (Luke 12:7). So we can admit each fear and let Him help us with them and fill us with His peace instead.

DEAR LORD, YOU KNOW EXACTLY THE REASONS I STRUGGLE WITH CERTAIN KINDS OF WORRIES AND FEARS. PLEASE COMFORT AND ENCOURAGE IN THE SPECIFIC WAYS I NEED SO THAT I CAN OVERCOME MY ANXIETY. AMEN.

Dealing with Regrets of the Past

Once we, too, were foolish and disobedient. We were misled and became slaves to many lusts and pleasures. Our lives were full of evil and envy, and we hated each other. But—When God our Savior revealed his kindness and love, he saved us, not because of the righteous things we had done, but because of his mercy. He washed away our sins, giving us a new birth and new life through the Holy Spirit.

TITUS 3:3–5 NLT

We might feel regret for things we've done in the past that we're not proud of, but we don't have to try to keep those things a secret from Jesus. We couldn't if we tried, because He sees all and knows all anyway (see, for example, Proverbs 15:3; Jeremiah 23:24; Hebrews 4:13). The Bible promises, "While we were still sinners, Christ died for us" (Romans 5:8 NIV). He didn't die for perfect people who have no sin. Those people don't even exist except for Jesus! He alone can offer us grace and salvation from sin because He did the work of suffering and dying on the cross to pay the price for our sin.

DEAR JESUS, THANK YOU THAT I DON'T HAVE TO KEEP ON THINKING OF MY REGRETS FROM THE PAST. I'M SORRY FOR THEM, I ASK YOU FOR FORGIVENESS FROM THEM, AND NOW I CAN BE DONE WITH THEM. YOU KNOW MY PAST AND YET YOU SAVED ME AND YOU LOVE ME AND GIVE ME NEW LIFE. I'M SO VERY GRATEFUL. AMEN.

Soar!

Have you never heard? Have you never understood? The Lord is the everlasting God, the Creator of all the earth. He never grows weak or weary. No one can measure the depths of his understanding. He gives power to the weak and strength to the powerless. Even youths will become weak and tired, and young men will fall in exhaustion. But those who trust in the Lord will find new strength. They will soar high on wings like eagles. They will run and not grow weary. They will walk and not faint.

Isaiah 40:28–31 NLT

When you feel exhausted, you have to take care of yourself and give your mind and body a break to rest! And you can remember that God has an endless supply of supernatural strength and energy. If schoolwork or tough friendships or a stressful family life or health problems or anything at all are draining you, take time to focus on this scripture. Wait patiently on God to come to your rescue and make you rise up with wings like an eagle! Can you picture that awesome imagery?

DEAR GOD, I AM SO, SO EXHAUSTED, AND I'M GLAD THAT YOU NEVER ARE. YOU KNOW WHAT IS GOING ON IN MY LIFE THAT'S SO DRAINING. PLEASE GIVE ME YOUR ENERGY, STRENGTH, AND COURAGE TO KEEP ON GOING AND TO OVERCOME. HELP ME SOAR HIGH ON WINGS LIKE AN EAGLE! AMEN.

When You're in Distress

Have mercy on me, Lord, for I am in distress. Tears blur my eyes. My body and soul are withering away. I am dying from grief; my years are shortened by sadness.
Psalm 31:9–10 NLT

Have you ever felt like this psalm describes? Maybe a "frenemy" is being mean to you. Maybe right now school seems too hard. Maybe a loved one has died or a close friend has moved away. Whenever you feel in deep distress, in those times when you feel like you'll never stop crying, be sure to cry out to God. He loves you and He is full of mercy toward you. This psalm goes on to say to God, "How great is the goodness you have stored up for those who fear you. You lavish it on those who come to you for protection, blessing them before the watching world. You hide them in the shelter of your presence, safe from those who conspire against them. You shelter them in your presence, far from accusing tongues. Praise the Lord, for he has shown me the wonders of his unfailing love" (Psalm 31:19–21 NLT).

DEAR LORD, THANK YOU FOR CARING ABOUT MY DISTRESS. I NEED YOUR LOVE AND MERCY SO MUCH. PLEASE SHOW ME THAT YOU SEE MY SADNESS AND STRUGGLES, AND GIVE ME HELP, COMFORT, AND STRENGTH TO OVERCOME. AMEN.

Let God Lead

I will give honor and thanks to the Lord, Who has told me what to do. Yes, even at night my mind teaches me. I have placed the Lord always in front of me. Because He is at my right hand, I will not be moved. And so my heart is glad. My soul is full of joy. My body also will rest without fear. For You will not give me over to the grave. And You will not allow Your Holy One to return to dust.

PSALM 16:7–10 NLV

Are you always putting the Lord in front of you? It's the best way to live! Think of the specific ways you are letting God lead, celebrate that with gratitude, and keep it up! Also, admit the ways you need to start letting Him lead. Because when the Lord is always in front of you and you stay on His path, you will be steady and stable in all your life—even when hard, sad, and painful times hit. No matter what comes your way, God will give you joy, peace, and rest without fear.

DEAR GOD, IT'S HARD SOMETIMES, BUT PLEASE HELP ME NOT TO WANT TO BE THE LEADER OF MY LIFE. I WANT TO BE ABLE TO HONESTLY SAY I ALWAYS PUT YOU IN FRONT OF ME. I KNOW YOU WILL LEAD ME FAR BETTER THAN I CAN LEAD BECAUSE YOU ARE PERFECT AND WORTHY OF ALL PRAISE! AMEN.

Have a Grateful Heart

As he was going into a village, ten men who had leprosy met him. They stood at a distance and called out in a loud voice, "Jesus, Master, have pity on us!" When he saw them, he said, "Go, show yourselves to the priests." And as they went, they were cleansed. One of them, when he saw he was healed, came back, praising God in a loud voice. He threw himself at Jesus' feet and thanked him—and he was a Samaritan. Jesus asked, "Were not all ten cleansed? Where are the other nine?"

LUKE 17:12–17 NIV

"Start each day with a grateful heart" is a lovely saying that maybe you've heard. This passage from Luke 17 reminds us of how important it is to be grateful and say thank you for our blessings, especially to Jesus. These ten men had been miraculously healed by Him. You'd think they would have been bursting with gratitude. Yet only one of them turned back to Jesus to say thank You and worship Him. In whatever ways God blesses us, we should always want to be like the one man and not the other nine!

DEAR JESUS, PLEASE FORGIVE ME IF I'VE EVER FORGOTTEN TO THANK YOU! I AM GRATEFUL FOR YOUR GIVING ME SALVATION AND LIFE, AND I WANT TO WORSHIP AND PRAISE YOU FOR EVERYTHING. AMEN.

Praise and Praise Some More!

Praise the Lord*! Praise God in his sanctuary; praise him in his mighty heavens! Praise him for his mighty deeds; praise him according to his excellent greatness! Praise him with trumpet sound; praise him with lute and harp! Praise him with tambourine and dance; praise him with strings and pipe! Praise him with sounding cymbals; praise him with loud clashing cymbals! Let everything that has breath praise the* Lord*! Praise the* Lord*!*

Psalm 150 ESV

Do you see a pattern and theme in Psalm 150? We're supposed to *praise the Lord*—everywhere, for everything, in all kinds of ways! Praise is good for our minds, bodies, and souls, because continually praising God means we are constantly aware of His greatness and power. When we focus on that greatness and power and how He loves and cares for us, we have nothing to fear or worry about.

DEAR GOD, YES, I PRAISE YOU! YOU TAKE CARE OF ALL MY NEEDS. YOU ARE GREATER AND MIGHTIER THAN ANY PROBLEM OR ENEMY I WILL EVER FACE. I HAVE NOTHING TO FEAR WHEN I'M PRAISING AND TRUSTING YOU! AMEN.

Unique Gifts

There are different kinds of spiritual gifts, but they all come from the same Spirit. There are different ways to serve the same Lord, and we can each do different things. Yet the same God works in all of us and helps us in everything we do.
1 CORINTHIANS 12:4–6 CEV

It's so cool that people are unique and have different God-given gifts and talents. Our world would be dull if everyone had the same personalities and abilities. The Bible talks about how the Holy Spirit gives different gifts to each of His people, different ways to serve Jesus, different ways to help one another. It's important not to compare and expect other Christians to be exactly like us. God purposefully made us all different, with plans and purposes specifically designed for us. We can let Him show us what they are and then do them for His glory!

DEAR LORD, THANK YOU FOR BLESSING ME WITH UNIQUE GIFTS, AND THANK YOU FOR BLESSING OTHERS AS WELL. HELP US NOT TO COMPARE BUT TO CELEBRATE AND PRAISE YOU FOR ALL OUR DIFFERENCES. HELP US TO KNOW HOW AND WHEN TO USE OUR GIFTS LIKE YOU WANT US TO. AMEN.

Don't Despise Discipline

Blessed is the one you discipline, Lord,
the one you teach from your law.
Psalm 94:12 NIV

For good mental self-care, don't despise discipline. You can trust that "the Lord disciplines those he loves" (Hebrews 12:6 NLT), and it's for your good. The Bible states very clearly that no one enjoys discipline while it's happening, but later "it produces a harvest of righteousness and peace for those who have been trained by it" (Hebrews 12:11 NIV). You know this in other areas of your life. If you're disciplined with your homework and studying, there's a reward of good grades and new knowledge and skills learned. If you're disciplined in sports or art or music, there's a reward in how you perform and create. And even more important than the good disciplines of this world are the ways God is spiritually disciplining us to grow in our faith and obedience to Him. We should "endure hardship as discipline; God is treating you as his children" (Hebrews 12:7 NIV). And "God disciplines us for our good, in order that we may share in his holiness" (Hebrews 12:10 NIV).

DEAR LORD, I'M GRATEFUL TO BE YOUR CHILD, SO HELP ME NEVER TO DESPISE DISCIPLINE. PLEASE KEEP UP THE GOOD THINGS YOU ARE DOING IN AND FOR ME SO THAT I CAN BE CLOSER TO YOU AND MORE LIKE YOU. AMEN.

Feed Yourself Well

Jesus was led by the Holy Spirit to a desert. There He was tempted by the devil. Jesus went without food for forty days and forty nights. After that He was hungry. The devil came tempting Him and said, "If You are the Son of God, tell these stones to be made into bread." But Jesus said, "It is written, 'Man is not to live on bread only. Man is to live by every word that God speaks.'"

MATTHEW 4:1–4 NLV

What happens if you haven't had enough to eat all day? You feel awful, right? Your stomach growls and hurts, and maybe your head hurts too. You probably feel tired and weak. We all need food, and we can't last too long without it. But even more importantly than food for our physical health, we need food for our spiritual and mental health. We find that kind of food in the truth of God's words. So just as we usually feed our bodies with breakfast, lunch, and dinner (and probably some good snacks in between!), we need to feed our hearts, minds, and spirits with God's good truth in the Bible to strengthen, nourish, and encourage us.

DEAR GOD, THANK YOU FOR YOUR AWESOME WORD TO GUIDE MY LIFE AND GIVE ME WISDOM, PEACE, HOPE, AND STRENGTH. REMIND ME THAT I CAN'T DO ANYTHING WELL UNLESS I'M SPIRITUALLY AND MENTALLY HEALTHY BY FEASTING ON YOUR WORD! AMEN.

When You're in a Storm

But soon a fierce storm came up. High waves were breaking into the boat, and it began to fill with water. Jesus was sleeping at the back of the boat with his head on a cushion. The disciples woke him up, shouting, "Teacher, don't you care that we're going to drown?" When Jesus woke up, he rebuked the wind and said to the waves, "Silence! Be still!" Suddenly the wind stopped, and there was a great calm. Then he asked them, "Why are you afraid? Do you still have no faith?"

MARK 4:37–40 NLT

Jesus' disciples were absolutely terrified during the storm described in Mark 4. Yet it took only a few words from Jesus to make everything okay. Through the Holy Spirit, that same powerful, storm-stopping presence of Jesus is with you this very moment! Whenever you're going through any hard thing, you can choose to call on Jesus and ask Him to make a way through the storm for you.

JESUS, YOU ARE CAPABLE OF SIMPLY SPEAKING THE WORDS AND CALMING ANYTHING DOWN. I CALL ON YOU NOW FOR YOUR HELP WITH THE STORM I'M FACING IN MY LIFE. AMEN.

So Much More Than Expected

When he had finished speaking, he said to Simon, "Put out into deep water, and let down the nets for a catch." Simon answered, "Master, we've worked hard all night and haven't caught anything. But because you say so, I will let down the nets." When they had done so, they caught such a large number of fish that their nets began to break. So they signaled their partners in the other boat to come and help them, and they came and filled both boats so full that they began to sink.

LUKE 5:4–7 NIV

Jesus' disciples had just spent the whole night fishing and had caught nothing, but Jesus only had to say the words, and suddenly they caught enough fish to tear their nets and sink their boats! When you're praying to God but haven't received an answer yet, remember that Jesus is able to bless you with much more than you expect. Keep learning about Him, keep trusting Him, keep praising Him, keep waiting on His perfect timing, and keep asking Him for everything you need—and He just might provide much more than you ever dreamed possible!

JESUS, HELP ME TO REMEMBER HOW YOU LOVE TO BLESS AND SURPRISE PEOPLE—INCLUDING ME—WITH MUCH MORE THAN EXPECTED SOMETIMES, IN ABOVE-AND-BEYOND KINDS OF WAYS! AMEN.

Don't Believe Lies About Jesus

Some of the guards went into the city and told the leading priests what had happened. A meeting with the elders was called, and they decided to give the soldiers a large bribe. They told the soldiers, "You must say, 'Jesus' disciples came during the night while we were sleeping, and they stole his body.' If the governor hears about it, we'll stand up for you so you won't get in trouble." So the guards accepted the bribe and said what they were told to say. Their story spread widely among the Jews, and they still tell it today.

MATTHEW 28:11–15 NLT

Keep your mind settled and strong in truth from God's Word for good mental health—and don't believe any lies about Jesus. Since there were so many eyewitnesses (read 1 Corinthians 15:5–7) to Jesus' resurrection, isn't it crazy how so many people didn't believe and still don't believe He actually rose to life again? We believe historical facts about all kinds of other things. But this was an astounding miracle, and our enemy Satan doesn't want people to believe in Jesus' resurrection and be saved from sins. This passage in Matthew shows us one way Satan deceived people—with a lie that was spread about Jesus' body being stolen. And sadly, that lie is still spreading today.

DEAR JESUS, I PRAY THAT PEOPLE WILL RECOGNIZE AND REJECT THE LIES THAT HAVE BEEN SPREAD ABOUT YOU. I PRAY FOR MORE AND MORE PEOPLE TO TRUST IN YOU AS THE ONE AND ONLY RISEN SAVIOR. AMEN.

Get Dressed in Godly Armor

Put on every piece of God's armor so you will be able to resist the enemy in the time of evil. Then after the battle you will still be standing firm. Stand your ground, putting on the belt of truth and the body armor of God's righteousness. For shoes, put on the peace that comes from the Good News so that you will be fully prepared. In addition to all of these, hold up the shield of faith to stop the fiery arrows of the devil. Put on salvation as your helmet, and take the sword of the Spirit, which is the word of God.

EPHESIANS 6:13–17 NLT

You've gotta get dressed for good self-care! Do you have certain clothes you like to wear because when you put them on, you instantly feel more confident? Maybe a favorite outfit that you know looks good and feels good too? An athlete ready to compete feels more confident and brave with her uniform and gear. And a soldier going to battle absolutely needs protective armor. God tells us that as Christians we need our best outfit on as well—a special kind of spiritual armor to wear as we fight the spiritual battles going on around us at all times.

DEAR GOD, THANK YOU FOR BLESSING AND EQUIPPING ME WITH PROTECTIVE ARMOR FROM YOU, WHICH IS EXACTLY WHAT I NEED TO BE EQUIPPED FOR ANY CHALLENGE OR BATTLE IN THIS WORLD. AMEN.

Your Best Isn't Good Enough—and That's Okay!

As they approached, Jesus said, "Now here is a genuine son of Israel—a man of complete integrity." "How do you know about me?" Nathanael asked. Jesus replied, "I could see you under the fig tree before Philip found you." Then Nathanael exclaimed, "Rabbi, you are the Son of God—the King of Israel!" Jesus asked him, "Do you believe this just because I told you I had seen you under the fig tree? You will see greater things than this."

John 1:47–50 NLT

Let this truth give you relief and peace today: Your best is never good enough. You might be wondering, *What? How is that relieving and peaceful?* Because you don't have to work your way to God with good deeds and a perfect personality, that's why. You simply have to trust in Jesus' work on the cross to pay the price for your sin and accept the free gift of grace He gives to those who accept Him. Take Nathanael, for example. Jesus described Nathanael as a man of "complete integrity." What a compliment from the only one who knows everything! Still, Nathanael needed to change his life to love and follow Jesus, just like we all do! It's wonderful to be a good and kind person, but even the most moral and nicest people still need to choose Jesus as Savior.

DEAR JESUS, HELP ME TO REMEMBER THAT ALL THE NICENESS IN THE WORLD DOESN'T BRING SALVATION. TRUSTING IN YOU AS THE ONE AND ONLY SAVIOR FROM SIN IS WHAT SAVES. HELP ME TO SHARE THIS TRUTH WITH OTHERS. AMEN.

Get Out in Nature

What may be known about God is plain to them, because God has made it plain to them. For since the creation of the world God's invisible qualities—his eternal power and divine nature—have been clearly seen, being understood from what has been made, so that people are without excuse.

ROMANS 1:19–20 NIV

Time outdoors in God's beautiful world of nature is absolutely essential for good self-care! God has shown Himself and His qualities through everything He has made in creation, so no person on earth can say they know nothing about God. We can see Him in the little details of flowers and in far-off sparkling stars in the clear nighttime skies. We can see Him in the amazing ways our human body systems are designed to work and keep us alive. We can see Him in the ways animals know how to hunt for their food and care for their young and build themselves a home. That names just a few! Our Creator God is awesome and worthy of all our praise!

DEAR GOD, IT'S SO GOOD FOR ME—MIND, BODY, AND SOUL—TO SEE YOUR QUALITIES IN ALL THE THINGS YOU HAVE MADE. THANK YOU FOR MAKING YOURSELF KNOWN. I PRAY THAT MORE PEOPLE WILL WANT TO GROW CLOSER TO YOU THROUGH JESUS BECAUSE OF SEEING YOU IN CREATION. AMEN.

Press Pause, Keep Your Cool

"You have heard that our ancestors were told, 'You must not murder. If you commit murder, you are subject to judgment.' But I say, if you are even angry with someone, you are subject to judgment! If you call someone an idiot, you are in danger of being brought before the court. And if you curse someone, you are in danger of the fires of hell."

MATTHEW 5:21–22 NLT

Lots of anger is not good for your mind and body. Jesus gave some very serious warnings about it, so it's obviously important that we don't let angry emotions overwhelm us and make us feel out of control. We shouldn't lash out with angry actions and name-calling and cursing. We constantly have to ask for Jesus' help to deal with anger wisely and well. If you feel anger taking over your mind and body, think of pressing pause and then breathing deeply to keep your cool. Look up more scriptures like these for help too:

> *A kind answer soothes angry feelings, but harsh words stir them up. (Proverbs 15:1 CEV)*

> *"Don't sin by letting anger control you." Don't let the sun go down while you are still angry, for anger gives a foothold to the devil. (Ephesians 4:26–27 NLT)*

DEAR JESUS, PLEASE GIVE ME WISDOM ABOUT ANGER AND HELP ME TO REMEMBER YOUR WARNINGS. HELP ME TO GET ANGRY ONLY ABOUT THINGS THAT MAKE YOU ANGRY, AND HELP ME TO KNOW WHAT GOOD AND HELPFUL THINGS TO DO WITH THAT ANGER. AMEN.

Be Well Watered

The Lord will guide you continually, giving you water when you are dry and restoring your strength. You will be like a well-watered garden, like an ever-flowing spring.

Isaiah 58:11 NLT

What are the things that dry you up and steal all your energy? What makes you feel worn out, weak, and exhausted sometimes? Lots of physical activity and very little sleep will do it, for sure. And what about on the inside? Sometimes we start to feel dry and ugly like dying plants when we aren't spending good time with Jesus. We need to read His Word and pray and worship Him so that He can revive us. He can give us living water so that we never feel dry and thirsty again!

DEAR JESUS, I NEED YOUR LIVING WATER EVERY DAY. THANK YOU FOR REFRESHING AND REVIVING ME! AMEN.

Focus on What God Can Do

Daniel said, "Let the name of God be honored forever and ever, for wisdom and power belong to Him. He changes the times and the years. He takes kings away, and puts kings in power. He gives wisdom to wise men and much learning to men of understanding. He makes known secret and hidden things. He knows what is in the darkness. Light is with Him. I give thanks and praise to You, O God of my fathers. For You have given me wisdom and power. Even now You have made known what we asked of You. You have made the king's dream known to us."

DANIEL 2:20–23 NLV

Daniel in the lions' den isn't just a cool Sunday school story. It's good for your mental health today too! It's a true account of great faith, prayer, obedience, and courage that we all need to read and remember again and again. This scripture in Daniel 2 is part of Daniel's prayer to God, worshipping Him for all the astonishing things He is able to do. Let it encourage you and strengthen you in mind and body, today and every day!

DEAR LORD, PLEASE HELP ME ALWAYS TO REMEMBER YOUR AWESOMENESS, ABILITIES, AND ACTIONS. I WANT TO WORSHIP YOU AND BE CONFIDENT BECAUSE I FOCUS ON YOUR POWER AND WORKS—PAST, PRESENT, AND FUTURE TOO. AMEN.

Cultivate Your Soil and Roots

Have your roots planted deep in Christ. Grow in Him. Get your strength from Him. Let Him make you strong in the faith as you have been taught. Your life should be full of thanks to Him.
COLOSSIANS 2:7 NLV

The deeper a plant's roots go, the stronger it is. And the deeper you grow roots into Jesus, the stronger you are too! Take a look at the parable Jesus taught in Luke 8, where He teaches about seeds and soils. He explained the parable this way:

> *"The seed is God's word. The seeds that fell on the footpath represent those who hear the message, only to have the devil come and take it away from their hearts and prevent them from believing and being saved. The seeds on the rocky soil represent those who hear the message and receive it with joy. But since they don't have deep roots, they believe for a while, then they fall away when they face temptation. The seeds that fell among the thorns represent those who hear the message, but all too quickly the message is crowded out by the cares and riches and pleasures of this life. And so they never grow into maturity. And the seeds that fell on the good soil represent honest, good-hearted people who hear God's word, cling to it, and patiently produce a huge harvest." (Luke 8:11–15 NLT)*

DEAR JESUS, PLEASE HELP ME TO CULTIVATE GOOD SOIL THAT PRODUCES A BIG HARVEST BECAUSE I CLING TO YOUR WORD. AMEN.

Safe in God's Love

But you, dear friends, must build each other up in your most holy faith, pray in the power of the Holy Spirit, and await the mercy of our Lord Jesus Christ, who will bring you eternal life. In this way, you will keep yourselves safe in God's love.

JUDE 20–21 NLT

Are you keeping yourself safe in God's love, like this scripture says? Let this list help you evaluate:

Do you regularly read God's Word to learn from Him?

Do you talk to Him through prayer and have quiet time to listen for answers?

Do you go to a Bible-teaching church to worship and learn and fellowship and serve there?

Do you have other strong Christians in your life who help remind you and encourage you in God's truth and love?

Do you fill your mind with songs of praise to Him?

These are all awesome ways to keep yourself safe in the love of God! Through His Holy Spirit, He never leaves you, but sometimes it gets easy to ignore that He is there. So remember to keep yourself safe in His love every moment of every day.

DEAR GOD, I WANT TO KEEP MYSELF SAFE IN YOUR LOVE, STAYING IN CLOSE RELATIONSHIP WITH YOU! PLEASE HELP ME NEVER TO FORGET OR IGNORE YOU. AMEN.

Don't Take Your Focus Off Jesus

Peter got out of the boat and walked on the water and came to Jesus.
MATTHEW 14:29 ESV

One time when Jesus went off to pray alone, His disciples were in a boat traveling on ahead of Him. Then in the middle of the night, He walked out on the lake to catch up with them. The disciples were terrified, thinking they were seeing a ghost! But Jesus said to them, "It's me! Don't be afraid." As soon as the disciple Peter realized it was Jesus out on the lake, he wanted to walk on water too. And he trusted that Jesus could make that happen. So Peter climbed out of the boat and miraculously started walking on the waves toward Jesus. But then something changed, and he began to sink. Peter had taken his focus off Jesus and put it on the wind and waves instead. The same thing will happen to us if we're not careful. We must keep looking to Jesus through every storm in life. If we do, He'll keep us steady. If we don't, we'll sink.

DEAR JESUS, I WANT TO BE STEADY IN LIFE, NOT SINKING BECAUSE OF THE MANY STORMS THAT WILL COME MY WAY. I WANT TO KEEP MY FOCUS ON YOU AND YOUR AWESOME POWER. PLEASE HELP ME! AMEN.

Let Go of Old, and Get Something New

There is one who is free in giving, and yet he grows richer.
And there is one who keeps what he should give, but he ends
up needing more. The man who gives much will have much,
and he who helps others will be helped himself.
PROVERBS 11:24–25 NLV

Do you think it's good and healthy to be a hoarder? Imagine if your room had absolutely no extra space because you never got rid of anything. Yikes! We have to be wise about what to keep and what to give away and get rid of. In a similar way, God wants us to hold not tightly but *lightly* to the blessings He has given us. We can't open our hands to receive new gifts from God if we won't let go of the things He has already given us. Our hands can't fit everything at once. And neither can our lives! So we are called to give and give and then give some more, and be amazed by the ways God gives us new gifts and blessings.

DEAR LORD, PLEASE HELP ME TO BE A GENEROUS GIVER, NOT A SELFISH HOARDER. I KNOW YOU WANT TO USE ME TO SHARE AND BLESS OTHERS WITH WHAT YOU'VE GIVEN ME. EVERYTHING I HAVE IS ULTIMATELY YOURS. I GIVE IT BACK TO YOU, AND I'M GRATEFUL FOR ALL I CONSTANTLY RECEIVE FROM YOU! AMEN.

The Lord Is Your Light, So Don't Be Afraid

The Lord is my light and my salvation—so why should I be afraid?
The Lord is my fortress, protecting me from danger, so why should I tremble?
When evil people come to devour me, when my enemies and foes attack
me, they will stumble and fall. Though a mighty army surrounds me,
my heart will not be afraid. Even if I am attacked, I will remain confident.

Psalm 27:1–3 NLT

No matter how old we get, sometimes we still hold on to some fears of the dark. Darkness holds uncertainty and also possibly hidden dangers—because we just can't see!—and that's why it can be a little scary. So be encouraged by Psalm 27 that says God is our light. We don't have to worry about the unknown because He knows it, and He saves us from any hidden dangers. We have nothing to fear with the Lord as our light, our Savior, and our strength.

DEAR GOD, THANK YOU THAT YOU ARE THE LIGHT, AND YOU ARE MY LIGHT. THERE IS NO DARKNESS WITH YOU, AND NOTHING IS HIDDEN FROM YOU OR UNKNOWN BY YOU. YOU SAVE ME AND GIVE ME STRENGTH AND COURAGE SO THAT I DON'T HAVE TO FEAR ANYONE OR ANYTHING. AMEN.

An Understanding Heart

"Give me an understanding heart so that I can govern your people well and know the difference between right and wrong. For who by himself is able to govern this great people of yours?" The Lord was pleased that Solomon had asked for wisdom.

1 Kings 3:9–10 NLT

King Solomon was the king who could ask God for anything at all, but he asked God for wisdom and an understanding heart. Solomon loved God and knew wisdom would be most valuable—because wanting to follow God's ways of right and wrong and wanting to lead others in God's wisdom matters forever, not just for a little while like the riches and possessions of this world. It takes strong intention and commitment to be someone who thinks about the things of heaven more than the things of earth (Colossians 3:2).

Let Solomon inspire you. Every time you find yourself faced with a choice either to focus on the things of the world or to focus on God's wise ways of right and wrong, choose God's good ways, which are always the very best ways for you—mind, body, and soul!

DEAR GOD, REMIND ME EVERY DAY OF KING SOLOMON. HELP ME TO ASK YOU FOR WISDOM LIKE HE DID. HELP ME TO USE YOUR PERFECT WISDOM FAITHFULLY IN ALL THINGS. AMEN.

You Are Beautiful, the Work of God's Hand

But now, O Lord, you are our Father; we are the clay, and you are our potter; we are all the work of your hand.
Isaiah 64:8 ESV

Do you remember drawing or painting something or sculpting something out of clay when you were little, and you knew exactly what it was meant to be, but no one else seemed to? That's because you were the creator, so of course you knew, even if no one else could see it. Never forget that the one true God is your Creator. Tell yourself regularly that you are the beautiful work of His hand. Sometimes you might not be sure exactly who you are meant to be and what you're supposed to be doing as you're growing and still figuring life out, but God always knows. Keep following Him and asking Him to guide you into the extraordinary life He made you for, full of the good things He has planned for you.

DEAR GOD, YOU ARE THE POTTER AND I AM THE CLAY. THANK YOU FOR MAKING ME AND HAVING GOOD PLANS FOR ME. PLEASE SHOW ME DAY BY DAY WHAT THOSE PLANS ARE. I WANT TO FOLLOW YOU FOREVER! AMEN.

So Much Better Than Okay!

We know that God makes all things work together for the good of those who love Him and are chosen to be a part of His plan.
ROMANS 8:28 NLV

"It's going to be okay." Have you ever heard those words and they gave you no comfort—they just made you want to scream? Sometimes it can feel like the person saying them to you during a rough time doesn't *truly* know or care about your problem and/or pain and how awful life feels in the midst of it. That's when remembering Romans 8:28 is so essential! If you love God, are trusting in Jesus as your Savior, and are living for Him, God is working in every kind of situation—even the hardest and weirdest and worst ones—and truly will make everything okay in the end. And not just okay but so much better than okay! Better than you can ever imagine in perfect paradise in heaven someday. It's understandable that we all sometimes feel like nothing will ever be okay again in this sinful and crazy world, and so we need to be reminded of the truth of God's Word every single day!

DEAR GOD, REMIND ME THAT YOU ARE ALWAYS WORKING FOR THE GOOD OF THOSE WHO LOVE YOU! I LOVE YOU, AND I TRUST YOU! PLEASE KEEP HOLDING TIGHT TO ME, ESPECIALLY WHEN I AM HURTING AND FEEL SO DISCOURAGED. HELP ME TO KEEP REACHING FOR YOU. AMEN.

What Are You Watching, Listening to, Thinking About?

Whatever is true, whatever is noble, whatever is right, whatever is pure, whatever is lovely, whatever is admirable—if anything is excellent or praiseworthy—think about such things. Whatever you have learned or received or heard from me, or seen in me— put it into practice. And the God of peace will be with you.

PHILIPPIANS 4:8–9 NIV

It may sound odd, but it's good to think about: If Jesus were physically in the room with you, would you be comfortable showing Him what you watch, read, and listen to on TV, online, in books and magazines, and through music and social media? It all matters. It all affects who you are and how you think and talk and act. It affects your mental health. The world will try to tell you even the bad stuff is all just for fun, but don't listen to the world; listen to God, especially through His Word. In the book of Philippians, the apostle Paul said to keep our minds thinking about what is true, noble, right, pure, lovely, admirable, excellent, and praiseworthy. Whenever you put a thought or idea into your mind from what you watch and read and listen to, ask yourself if it matches up with Philippians 4:8–9!

DEAR GOD, HELP ME TO BE CAREFUL ABOUT WHAT I ALLOW INTO MY MIND THROUGH THE MANY FORMS OF ENTERTAINMENT AND MEDIA IN THE WORLD. I WANT TO OBEY YOU AND YOUR WORD AND HONOR YOU WITH MY CHOICES, PLUS PROTECT MY MENTAL HEALTH! AMEN.

Physical Training vs. Godliness

Train yourself to be godly. "Physical training is good, but training for godliness is much better, promising benefits in this life and in the life to come." This is a trustworthy saying, and everyone should accept it. This is why we work hard and continue to struggle, for our hope is in the living God, who is the Savior of all people and particularly of all believers.

1 TIMOTHY 4:7–10 NLT

There are many popular ways to keep your body in good shape these days, so many workout plans and diets to follow. And that's all great! Exercise and eating right are important, and the Bible tells us that we definitely should take good care of our bodies (see 1 Corinthians 6:19–20). But even more important, the Bible tells us that we should grow in godliness. We should strive to learn more and more about God and to live like His Son, Jesus. Physical fitness here on earth matters for a little while, but growing strong in knowing and loving God matters forever.

DEAR GOD, I WANT TO BE IN THE RIGHT KIND OF SHAPE. PLEASE HELP ME NOT ONLY TO BE PHYSICALLY FIT BUT, MORE IMPORTANTLY, TO BE SPIRITUALLY FIT BY LEARNING AND GROWING CLOSER AND CLOSER TO YOU. AMEN.

Don't Ever Let Yourself Drift Away

So we must listen very carefully to the truth we have heard, or we may drift away from it. For the message God delivered through angels has always stood firm, and every violation of the law and every act of disobedience was punished. So what makes us think we can escape if we ignore this great salvation that was first announced by the Lord Jesus himself and then delivered to us by those who heard him speak? And God confirmed the message by giving signs and wonders and various miracles and gifts of the Holy Spirit whenever he chose.

HEBREWS 2:1–4 NLT

♡

You may know people who used to trust in Jesus and the Bible who have now drifted away. Isn't it sad and discouraging when someone forgets God's truths or just doesn't care about loving and following Jesus anymore? We need to pray for those people and be careful never to let ourselves do the same and drift away from our love of God's Word and our willingness to learn from it. It truly is a lamp for our feet and a light for our path (Psalm 119:105). Without it, we are lost in this world and headed for all kinds of trouble.

DEAR GOD, I WANT TO FOLLOW YOU AND YOUR WORD ALWAYS. PLEASE PULL ME BACK QUICKLY AND HELP ME LISTEN TO YOU AGAIN IF I EVER START TO DRIFT AWAY. AMEN.

Prioritize, and Don't Idolize Anything but Jesus

"Worship the Lord your God, and serve him only."
MATTHEW 4:10 NIV

Flee from the worship of idols.
1 CORINTHIANS 10:14 NLT

You have to prioritize in life if you want to have good health and self-care. And you can't idolize anything but Jesus. When you hear the words *idolize* and *idol*, do you think of some big stone statue in ancient times? It may seem ridiculous to those of us who love Jesus to think it possible to have an idol. Why would anyone worship some object made of metal or stone that just sits there? But did you know that idols can actually be anything that we put above Jesus on our list of priorities? Jesus wants us to focus on Him first and then let all the other good things in our lives—like our family and friends, our church and activities, our schoolwork and jobs, our fun possessions like our phones, music, clothes, and jewelry—fall into place in good order, using His wisdom about them. When He is first, He helps us succeed the best ways possible with everything else.

DEAR JESUS, I'M GRATEFUL FOR ALL THE GOOD THINGS IN MY LIFE, BUT I DON'T WANT TO WORSHIP THEM. I WORSHIP YOU ALONE. PLEASE HELP ME TO STICK TO THIS PROMISE. AMEN.

Delight in Obeying God's Commands

Praise the Lord! How joyful are those who fear the Lord and delight in obeying his commands. Their children will be successful everywhere; an entire generation of godly people will be blessed. They themselves will be wealthy, and their good deeds will last forever. Light shines in the darkness for the godly. They are generous, compassionate, and righteous. Good comes to those who lend money generously and conduct their business fairly. Such people will not be overcome by evil. Those who are righteous will be long remembered. They do not fear bad news; they confidently trust the Lord to care for them. They are confident and fearless and can face their foes triumphantly.

Psalm 112:1–8 NLT

Do you fear the Lord and delight in His commands? That's how we have true joy and the promise of God's care and blessing. The words in Psalm 112 are something every Christian should want to be said of them. God doesn't want bad attitudes; He wants us to enjoy obeying Him because His commands are the wisest and best way to live a good life here on earth and then a perfect life in heaven. Loving God and obeying Him happily make us truly blessed, both now and forever.

DEAR LORD, THANK YOU FOR YOUR GOOD COMMANDS FOR ME TO FOLLOW. I ALWAYS WANT TO BE HAPPY TO OBEY THEM! AMEN.

Jesus Needed Self-Care Too

It was necessary for [Jesus] to be made in every respect like us, his brothers and sisters, so that he could be our merciful and faithful High Priest before God. Then he could offer a sacrifice that would take away the sins of the people. Since he himself has gone through suffering and testing, he is able to help us when we are being tested.

HEBREWS 2:17–18 NLT

It's wonderful that we have a Savior who knows about the need for self-care. He was human too. So He knows everything we go through, good times and bad. He "understands our weaknesses, for he faced all of the same testings we do" (Hebrews 4:15 NLT). When we think about that, it can help us feel closer to Him and stronger in our faith in Him. We can pray like this:

DEAR JESUS, I BELIEVE YOU FULLY UNDERSTAND WHAT IT'S LIKE TO BE HUMAN. YOU CAN RELATE TO ALL MY STRUGGLES AND FEARS, AND KNOWING THAT YOU RELATE HELPS ME BE HEALTHY AND STRONG AS I DEPEND ON YOU FOR HELP AND COMFORT. I TRUST THAT THE HOLY SPIRIT IS IN ME TO LEAD AND GUIDE ME THROUGH EVERY HARD THING. I TRUST THAT YOU KNOW, YOU CARE, AND YOU LOVE ME. AMEN.

Get Inspired by the Proverbs 31 Woman

She is more precious than rubies.
PROVERBS 31:10 NLT

The woman described in Proverbs 31 can be a great example to every woman, young or old, whether she marries and becomes a wife like that woman or not. She was a hard worker and full of integrity! Let these verses especially inspire you: "She is clothed with strength and dignity, and she laughs without fear of the future. When she speaks, her words are wise, and she gives instructions with kindness. She carefully watches everything in her household and suffers nothing from laziness. Her children stand and bless her. Her husband praises her: 'There are many virtuous and capable women in the world, but you surpass them all!' Charm is deceptive, and beauty does not last; but a woman who fears the LORD will be greatly praised" (Proverbs 31:25–30 NLT).

DEAR GOD, THANK YOU FOR SHOWING ME THE EXAMPLE OF THIS WOMAN IN YOUR WORD. I WANT TO DO MY BEST TO LIVE A LIFE LIKE SHE DID—WORKING HARD, LOVING AND INSPIRING THOSE AROUND ME, AND MOSTLY BRINGING PRAISE TO YOU! AMEN.

Be Careful About Money

For the love of money is the root of all kinds of evil. And some people, craving money, have wandered from the true faith and pierced themselves with many sorrows.
1 TIMOTHY 6:10 NLT

Having plenty of money and not having to worry much about finances or budget is a huge blessing and makes a lot of self-care really easy. But if we find ourselves to be so fortunate with plenty of money, we have to be very, very careful. First Timothy 6:17–18 (NIV) gives special instruction to the wealthy, saying, "Command those who are rich in this present world not to be arrogant nor to put their hope in wealth, which is so uncertain, but to put their hope in God, who richly provides us with everything for our enjoyment. Command them to do good, to be rich in good deeds, and to be generous and willing to share."

Our goals in life shouldn't be all about making lots of money. Our goals should focus on asking God for His will to be done in our lives. If He does happen to bless us with wealth, that's awesome—and we then get to be good stewards who are very generous with our wealth for His glory and to help spread the good news of Jesus.

DEAR LORD, THANK YOU FOR PROVIDING ME WITH MONEY. WHATEVER AMOUNTS I HAVE IN VARIOUS SEASONS OF LIFE, PLEASE GIVE ME WISDOM ABOUT MONEY AND WEALTH. I KNOW IT ALL ULTIMATELY COMES FROM YOU, AND I WANT TO USE WHATEVER YOU BLESS ME WITH TO PLEASE YOU AND POINT OTHERS TO YOU. AMEN.

Run Your Race Well

All these many people who have had faith in God are around us like a cloud. Let us put every thing out of our lives that keeps us from doing what we should. Let us keep running in the race that God has planned for us. Let us keep looking to Jesus. Our faith comes from Him and He is the One Who makes it perfect. He did not give up when He had to suffer shame and die on a cross. He knew of the joy that would be His later. Now He is sitting at the right side of God.

HEBREWS 12:1–2 NLV

The Bible says God has a race marked out for you. He has planned the course of your life, and if you keep looking to Jesus, He will lead you on it. As you keep looking to Him, you also have to regularly get rid of and avoid anything in your life that tries to pull you off the track and away from following Him. So it's extremely important to keep reading the Bible and learning from others who love and follow Jesus—at church and in your family and friendships.

DEAR JESUS, THANK YOU FOR PLANNING THE COURSE OF MY LIFE, THE RACE I SHOULD RUN. PLEASE KEEP ME GROWING CONSTANTLY STRONGER AND HEALTHIER IN MY FAITH IN YOU! AMEN.

When All Seems to Be Going Wrong

We are hard pressed on every side, but not crushed; perplexed, but not in despair; persecuted, but not abandoned; struck down, but not destroyed.

2 Corinthians 4:8–9 NIV

We need to take extraspecial care on days when every single thing on every side seems to be going wrong. Maybe we even have weeks or months like that—times when we feel so discouraged that we wonder when God is *ever* going to step in to help rescue us or at least protect us from any more trouble. This scripture promises that no matter how discouraged we feel, God will never let us get to a point where we cannot handle our discouragement. Sometimes He will wait to the last moment, but He will always provide a way out. He lets us experience hard things at times to teach us new lessons and show us how strong we can be in all kinds of situations when we depend on Him.

DEAR LORD, PLEASE HELP ME TO KEEP HANGING IN THERE AND HOLDING ON TO MY HOPE AND TRUST IN YOU WHEN I FEEL DISCOURAGED AND CONFUSED AND IN PAIN. I KNOW YOU WILL NEVER ABANDON ME, AND YOU HAVE GOOD PLANS AND BLESSINGS FOR ME. AMEN.

The Sufferings of This Present Time. . .

The sufferings of this present time are not worth comparing with the glory that is to be revealed to us.
ROMANS 8:18 ESV

Sometimes when we're struggling with a problem, need, or heartache, God does not just suddenly fix things like we hope. We sure wish He would, and we cry out to Him, asking Him to see our needs and make everything right again immediately. And when He doesn't, our trust in Him can really be shaken. We wonder why, and we question Him. Maybe we even feel anger and blame toward Him—but that anger and blame are not good to hold on to. Even when we're confused and hurting and frustrated over a prayer that seems to go unanswered, we need to look for the ways God is answering other prayers and showing His love in many other ways at the same time. We can continue to trust and know that we're blessed even through the hardest times. We can't possibly see all the good things God is doing in the midst of suffering, but one day in heaven we will understand. Then God will make all things perfect and new.

DEAR GOD, PLEASE HELP ME TO KEEP TRUSTING YOU EVEN WHEN I'M HURTING AND CONFUSED ABOUT WHAT YOU'RE DOING. WHEN I DON'T SEE YOU ANSWERING MY PRAYERS LIKE I HOPE, PLEASE REMIND ME OF HOW YOU ARE CARING FOR ME AND BLESSING ME IN OTHER WAYS. AMEN.

Don't Worry About What to Say

"I am sending you out like sheep among wolves. Therefore be as shrewd as snakes and as innocent as doves. Be on your guard; you will be handed over to the local councils and be flogged in the synagogues. On my account you will be brought before governors and kings as witnesses to them and to the Gentiles. But when they arrest you, do not worry about what to say or how to say it. At that time you will be given what to say, for it will not be you speaking, but the Spirit of your Father speaking through you."

MATTHEW 10:16–20 NIV

Sometimes the anxiety that affects our mental health comes from worrying what we will say in conflict situations. We can remember what Jesus told His disciples about going out into dangerous situations where people would hate them because they were His followers. Enemies would not want them to share the good news about Jesus. But Jesus encouraged His friends not to worry about what others would say. He promised them that they would have exactly the right words because the Spirit of God would speak through them. The Spirit of God can speak through you too!

DEAR GOD, PLEASE EASE MY ANXIETY AND SPEAK THROUGH ME AS YOU WANT TO. HELP ME TO SHARE YOUR TRUTH AND LOVE WHEREVER AND WHENEVER YOU WANT BECAUSE I TRUST YOU WILL GIVE ME ALL THE RIGHT WORDS. AMEN.

Don't Avoid and Delay

Give all your cares to the Lord and He will give you strength.
He will never let those who are right with Him be shaken.
PSALM 55:22 NLV

Have you ever tried to avoid what makes you anxious or afraid? We all can probably think of examples. Take a minute and consider if avoiding or procrastinating really helped, though. Were your fears and anxieties relieved or just delayed? Usually we should confront our fears, ask God for extra courage, and then face the tasks or problems fearlessly in God's power. If we do that, we won't have the worry of them hanging around in our minds for far too long.

When you find yourself regularly worried or scared, ask God to help you confront the fears rather than avoid them. Facing them directly will let you see how God's power can work through you to overcome! He loves you and wants to help you with everything! First Peter 5:7 (NIV) says, "Cast all your anxiety on him because he cares for you." Not just a little or some of it—but *all* of it!

DEAR GOD, WITH YOU WORKING IN ME, I WANT TO FACE MY FEARS AND WORRIES, NOT TRY TO AVOID OR DELAY THEM. PLEASE GIVE ME COURAGE AND HELP ME! THANK YOU FOR WANTING TO TAKE AWAY ALL MY ANXIETY. AMEN.

Be Ready for Jesus

The Spirit teaches you everything you need to know, and what he teaches is true—it is not a lie. So just as he has taught you, remain in fellowship with Christ. And now, dear children, remain in fellowship with Christ so that when he returns, you will be full of courage and not shrink back from him in shame.

1 John 2:27–28 NLT

As Christians, we're supposed to be ready for Jesus to return to earth at any moment (look up Matthew 24:44 and Luke 12:40, for example). To some people, that might give them anxiety, but for those of us who love Jesus and stay close to Him, it should be exciting! It should fill us with hope and joy! God's Word promises that if we remain in fellowship with Jesus, then we will be full of courage and not shrink back with fear or be ashamed in any way when Jesus returns to earth.

DEAR JESUS, I BELIEVE YOU WILL RETURN RIGHT ON YOUR PERFECT SCHEDULE. I'M WATCHING AND WAITING! I WANT TO STAY CLOSE TO YOU. AMEN.

"No Worries"

"That is why I tell you not to worry about everyday life—whether you have enough food and drink, or enough clothes to wear. . . . Look at the birds. They don't plant or harvest or store food in barns, for your heavenly Father feeds them. And aren't you far more valuable to him than they are? Can all your worries add a single moment to your life? And why worry about your clothing? Look at the lilies of the field and how they grow. They don't work or make their clothing. . . . Why do you have so little faith? So don't worry about these things, saying, 'What will we eat? What will we drink? What will we wear?' These things dominate the thoughts of unbelievers, but your heavenly Father already knows all your needs. Seek the Kingdom of God above all else, and live righteously, and he will give you everything you need. So don't worry about tomorrow, for tomorrow will bring its own worries. Today's trouble is enough for today."

MATTHEW 6:25–28, 30–34 NLT

"No worries" is a very common and nice thing to say (and sometimes not actually mean it), but the only one who can truly bless us with no worries is our good heavenly Father who cares the very most about us—even more than our closest friends and loved ones. If He knows and takes good care of even the birds and the flowers that He created, He definitely takes even better care of the people He made in His own image.

DEAR GOD, I'M GRATEFUL I CAN COME TO YOU AND HAVE TRULY NO WORRIES WHEN I FOCUS ON YOUR GREAT BIG LOVE AND YOUR ALL-KNOWING CARE FOR ME. AMEN.

Do Not Let Your Hearts Be Troubled

"Do not let your heart be troubled. You have put your trust in God, put your trust in Me also. There are many rooms in My Father's house. If it were not so, I would have told you. I am going away to make a place for you. After I go and make a place for you, I will come back and take you with Me. Then you may be where I am. You know where I am going and you know how to get there." Thomas said to Jesus, "Lord, we do not know where You are going. How can we know the way to get there?" Jesus said, "I am the Way and the Truth and the Life. No one can go to the Father except by Me."

JOHN 14:1–6 NLV

The stuff going on in our lives and our homes is really tough sometimes. Or the stuff we hear about from friends and classmates. But no matter what those circumstances are, we have to keep remembering and trusting Jesus' words and promises and sharing them with others. We hold on to great hope in our forever home. And Jesus is our Way, Truth, and Life until we get there.

DEAR JESUS, WHEN TROUBLES FEEL TOO MUCH AND LIFE FEELS SO HARD, PLEASE KEEP ME HOLDING ON TO YOUR PROMISES, AND HELP MY HEART TO NOT BE TROUBLED. PLEASE LEAD ME AND HELP ME TO PRESS ON WITH JOY BECAUSE YOU ARE THE ONE TRUE SAVIOR AND YOU'RE MAKING A PLACE IN PERFECT PARADISE FOR ME AND EVERYONE WHO TRUSTS IN YOU! AMEN.

When You Fear the Worst

God is our refuge and strength, always ready to help in times of trouble. So we will not fear when earthquakes come and the mountains crumble into the sea. Let the oceans roar and foam. Let the mountains tremble as the waters surge! A river brings joy to the city of our God, the sacred home of the Most High. God dwells in that city; it cannot be destroyed. From the very break of day, God will protect it. The nations are in chaos, and their kingdoms crumble! God's voice thunders, and the earth melts! The LORD of Heaven's Armies is here among us; the God of Israel is our fortress.

PSALM 46:1–7 NLT

Sometimes our mental health suffers because we imagine the worst that can happen, and then we focus on that. So we need this scripture to remind us that there is no horrible thing we can think of that God cannot deal with. He is always our help when we are in trouble no matter how awful the trouble is. Instead of imagining the worst, we should always think of the best—that God is our refuge and strength in all things!

DEAR GOD, WHEN MY MIND WANDERS TO WORST-CASE SCENARIOS, REMIND ME THAT YOU ARE MY REFUGE FROM EVEN THE WORST KIND OF TROUBLE. YOU GIVE ME SUPERNATURAL PEACE AND SECURITY. I LOVE YOU AND DEPEND ON YOU! AMEN.

When You Don't Feel Like Enough

It was by faith that even Sarah was able to have a child, though she was barren and was too old. She believed that God would keep his promise. And so a whole nation came from this one man who was as good as dead—a nation with so many people that, like the stars in the sky and the sand on the seashore, there is no way to count them. All these people died still believing what God had promised them. They did not receive what was promised, but they saw it all from a distance and welcomed it.

HEBREWS 11:11–13 NLT

If you're ever feeling not good enough, not pretty enough, not popular enough, not smart enough. . .or simply not enough, go to Hebrews 11 to see examples of Bible heroes who did amazing things—not because of who they were or how good, pretty, popular, or smart they were, but because they had great faith in God. Let their examples help you believe in God's power and might and His ability to do absolutely anything in and through you when you are humble and eager to do His will.

DEAR GOD, REMIND ME THAT I AM LOVED BY YOU AND I AM EXACTLY ENOUGH FOR THE AWESOME PLANS YOU CREATED ME FOR. WITH YOUR SPIRIT WORKING IN ME, PLEASE USE ME IN WONDERFUL WAYS FOR YOUR WILL AND YOUR GLORY. AMEN.

Honesty Is Self-Care

The Lord detests lying lips, but he delights in those who tell the truth.
Proverbs 12:22 NLT

If we choose to lie a lot or even a little, we're not taking good care of ourselves. Lies will catch up to us eventually, and we will face consequences. Not only that, but the world seems to get more and more confused about what truth even means, so we have to continue to stand strong and depend on Jesus for real truth. And since He hates lying lips, then so should we! And that means we should tell the truth about everything—big things and little things. In Luke 16:10 (NLT), Jesus said, "If you are faithful in little things, you will be faithful in large ones. But if you are dishonest in little things, you won't be honest with greater responsibilities." When we tell the truth, people can trust us, and Jesus will bless us.

DEAR LORD, PLEASE HELP ME TO LOVE THE TRUTH AND NOT TO LIE, EVEN ABOUT LITTLE THINGS. IF I MESS UP WITH THIS, HELP ME TO CONFESS AND MAKE THINGS RIGHT WITH YOUR WISDOM. I WANT TO BE AN HONEST AND TRUSTWORTHY PERSON. AMEN.

Good Mentors for Good Mental Health

Be imitators of me, as I am of Christ.
1 Corinthians 11:1 ESV

You need good mentors for good mental health. These are people who have lived longer than you who can help you through the stages of life ahead since they have already been there, done that. They should be people who love and follow Jesus so that they teach you more about loving and following Him too. So think about the people in your life who you admire the most and who love and follow Jesus. What is it about them? Is it their job? Is it their talents? Is it how they treat you and other people? Ask them good questions, like how they got into the job or activities they are in. Ask what it was like to endure the hard things they've gone through in life. Be willing and happy to have good and deep conversations so that you can learn lessons from those who are older and wiser than you.

DEAR LORD, PLEASE SHOW ME WISE PEOPLE WHO LOVE AND FOLLOW YOU, WHOM YOU WANT ME TO ADMIRE AND LEARN FROM. HELP ME TO DEVELOP MENTORING KIND OF RELATIONSHIPS WITH THEM AND HAVE IN-DEPTH CONVERSATIONS. THANK YOU FOR THEIR IMPACT ON MY LIFE! AMEN.

When You Have to Break It Off

Don't befriend angry people or associate with hot-tempered people, or you will learn to be like them and endanger your soul.
PROVERBS 22:24–25 NLT

Sometimes you just have to break away from a bad friendship or relationships to take good care of yourself. If someone you're close to starts making lots of wrong choices or treating you or others badly, it's not good to stay close to them. You don't want them to drag you down and into sin or trouble. God's Word certainly tells us to share love and kindness and love our enemies, but don't forget that it also says, "Bad company corrupts good character" (1 Corinthians 15:33 NLT). We all need wisdom to know how to show love to others without also joining in sin. And sometimes the bravest thing to do is to peacefully but firmly say to someone, "We just can't be friends or be together anymore."

DEAR GOD, PLEASE GIVE ME WISDOM ABOUT FRIENDSHIPS AND RELATIONSHIPS. SHOW ME IF I NEED TO END SOMETHING UNHEALTHY FOR ME THAT'S LEADING ME AWAY FROM CLOSE RELATIONSHIP WITH YOU. HELP ME TO BE BRAVE AND STRONG AND CONFIDENT WITH YOUR MIGHTY POWER. AMEN.

Make the Best Use of Your Time

So be careful how you live. Live as men who are wise and not foolish. Make the best use of your time. These are sinful days.
EPHESIANS 5:15–16 NLV

When we don't manage our time wisely, it's not good self-care. It causes all kinds of unnecessary stress! Have you ever experienced this? Maybe you put off a project that was due or procrastinated on studying for a big exam—and then found yourself cramming at the last minute. Nearly everyone has done this kind of thing. It's super easy to get distracted or to be lazy about doing the good work God has for us to do. What are the things that tempt you away from your responsibilities? Maybe time with friends, social media, music, and TV? Ask God to help you have good self-discipline and self-control with those things. Then ask Him to show you how to live carefully and wisely, making the best use of your time and using your gifts to glorify Him in all the things He has planned for you to do.

DEAR GOD, HELP ME TO MANAGE MY TIME WISELY TO ACCOMPLISH THE THINGS I NEED TO DO AND THE GOOD THINGS YOU CREATED ME FOR SO I CAN BRING GLORY TO YOU! AMEN.

Remind Yourself How Awesome and Blessed You Are!

See what great love the Father has lavished on us, that we should be called children of God! And that is what we are! The reason the world does not know us is that it did not know him. Dear friends, now we are children of God, and what we will be has not yet been made known.

1 JOHN 3:1–2 NIV

Sometimes you feel hopeless and discouraged for no good reason. Can you relate? It might be because you've forgotten who you are—how awesome and blessed you are as God's child. In times like that you especially need to go to scripture and remind yourself of these awesome truths:

You are made in the image of God (Genesis 1:27).

You are wonderfully made (Psalm 139:14).

You are God's masterpiece (Ephesians 2:10).

When you have accepted Jesus as your Savior, you are a child of God and you are filled with the powerful Holy Spirit (John 1:12; Romans 8:11).

You are royalty (1 Peter 2:9).

DEAR GOD, HELP ME NOT TO FORGET THAT I'M YOUR CHILD AND YOU ARE MY HEAVENLY FATHER WHO CREATED ME ON PURPOSE AND LOVES ME UNCONDITIONALLY. THANK YOU! PLEASE FILL ME WITH HOPE AND JOY AND CONFIDENCE. I'M HOLDING ON TO YOU AND NEVER WANT TO LET GO. PLEASE LEAD AND GUIDE ME ALL OF MY DAYS. AMEN.

Look for the Lord and Have Great Joy

Give great honor to the Lord with me. Let us praise His name together. I looked for the Lord, and He answered me. And He took away all my fears. They looked to Him and their faces shined with joy. Their faces will never be ashamed. This poor man cried, and the Lord heard him. And He saved him out of all his troubles. The angel of the Lord stays close around those who fear Him, and He takes them out of trouble.

PSALM 34:3–7 NLV

Name the worries and fears that are in your life right now. Do they go away if you focus on them? How could they? They grow bigger in your mind if you let them have lots of room in there. So don't give them room. Instead, give God lots of room in your brain. Look for Him and focus on Him—through reading His Word, singing praises to Him, praying to Him, making note of the way you see Him working in your life, and so on. Ask Him to show Himself to you in all kinds of ways. Then watch for how He pushes away your fears and helps with your worries and how He makes your face shine with joy!

DEAR GOD, PLEASE HELP ME TO TAKE MY FOCUS OFF MY FEARS AND PUT MY FOCUS ON YOU INSTEAD. FILL MY MIND AND HEART WITH JOY BECAUSE OF THOUGHTS OF YOU AND PRAISE TO YOU! AMEN.

The Good Kind of Pain

God's Word is living and powerful. It is sharper than a sword that cuts both ways. It cuts straight into where the soul and spirit meet and it divides them. It cuts into the joints and bones. It tells what the heart is thinking about and what it wants to do.

HEBREWS 4:12 NLV

This scripture about God's Word sounds painful, but that doesn't mean it's bad for you. Think of other things that are painful but good for you—like getting a good workout in sports or dance, which can be painful to muscles but good and healthy in the long run as you strengthen your body and build skill and endurance.

God's Word *can* be painful, but it is *always* good for us. It's painful when it's telling us what we're doing wrong and how we need to change. But if we follow it, we will be much healthier in the long run. So ask God to help you not to be afraid of the good kind of pain the Bible causes when it's helping you get rid of sin in your life. Then let God fill up those empty places with His goodness and love.

DEAR GOD, I WANT YOUR WORD TO HELP TAKE GOOD CARE OF ME, EVEN IF IT'S PAINFUL AT TIMES. CORRECT ME AND TEACH ME AND MAKE ME HEALTHY AND STRONGER AS I GROW CLOSER TO YOU AND OBEY YOU. AMEN.

God Created, God Controls, and God Protects

"When you pass through the waters, I will be with you. When you pass through the rivers, they will not flow over you. When you walk through the fire, you will not be burned. The fire will not destroy you. For I am the Lord your God, the Holy One of Israel, Who saves you."
ISAIAH 43:2–3 NLV

Our mental health can be affected when we hear of and learn about natural disasters. Things like volcanic eruptions, tidal waves, earthquakes, lightning strikes, hurricanes, tornadoes, and wildfires are fascinating—but really frightening too. No human being can control them or stop them from happening; we can only study them, watch out for them, and make emergency plans for safety during them. Natural disasters should be a reminder to people that no matter how great and smart we humans think we are, we can never truly control the earth or weather. So we should always respect the one true God who *can* control it all because He created it all. Even if natural disasters make us fearful or anxious, we can have peace knowing that our good God loves and protects His children with the promise of eternal life.

DEAR GOD, NO MATTER WHAT HAPPENS HERE ON EARTH WITH NATURAL DISASTERS, I KNOW THAT YOU ARE AN AWESOME CREATOR, AND I TRUST IN YOUR LOVE AND CARE! AMEN.

Let the Light Shine Bright!

He called you out of the darkness into his wonderful light.
1 PETER 2:9 NLT

It's important to let the light that is in us because of Jesus shine so brightly that others might leave the darkness and come to know Him too. We need to show others that we are different from the dark world around us. Ephesians 4:17–24 (CEV) states it with strong, straightforward words:

> *Stop living like stupid, godless people. Their minds are in the dark, and they are stubborn and ignorant and have missed out on the life that comes from God. They no longer have any feelings about what is right, and they are so greedy they do all kinds of indecent things. But this isn't what you were taught about Jesus Christ. He is the truth, and you heard about him and learned about him. You were told that your foolish desires will destroy you and that you must give up your old way of life with all its bad habits. Let the Spirit change your way of thinking and make you into a new person.*

JESUS, PLEASE HELP ME TO TURN FROM ANYTHING THAT IS OF THE DARKNESS AND LIVE IN YOUR WONDERFUL LIGHT. HELP ME TO SHINE IT SO BRIGHTLY SO THAT OTHERS ARE POINTED AWAY FROM SINFUL THINGS AND TOWARD YOU AS THEIR ONLY SAVIOR TOO. AMEN.

Seek God's Approval Above All

I'm not trying to win the approval of people, but of God.
If pleasing people were my goal, I would not be Christ's servant.
GALATIANS 1:10 NLT

We often worry *way* too much about getting the approval of other people, and that's not good for our mental health. To want approval means you want to be accepted and liked. And it's hard not to want that when you desire to have friends and get along well with others. But God's Word shows us that we shouldn't be looking for approval from people. We should look for God's approval most of all. If you start praying now to be God pleaser and a servant of Jesus—not a people pleaser—you'll take good care of yourself in many ways! You won't be so worried about what other people think of you. You won't want to give in to peer pressure. You'll be true to the unique, amazing person God designed you to be and follow the good plans He has for you. Yes, living for God's approval instead of people's can be challenging. But if you ask Him, God will help you keep your focus on Him; and at the same time, He'll be filling your life with the good and loving relationships you need with others.

DEAR GOD, I LOVE YOU MOST OF ALL, AND I DESIRE YOUR APPROVAL ABOVE ALL. IT'S A STRUGGLE NOT TO BE A PEOPLE PLEASER SOMETIMES, THOUGH. BUT I'M TRUSTING YOU WILL HELP ME. THANK YOU! AMEN.

Sweat It Out and Pray It Out!

Pray in the Spirit at all times and on every occasion. Stay alert and be persistent in your prayers for all believers everywhere.
Ephesians 6:18 NLT

Do you ever pray while you take a long walk or a nice run? Or during any type of exercise or workout? Exercise is such a great way to relieve anxiety, stress, and worries. And adding prayer time into your workout makes it even better! As you sweat it out in whatever your favorite form of exercise is, focus your mind on bringing your needs and the needs of others before God. Spend time praising and thanking Him too! Ask Him to let any anxiety pour out of you along with all that perspiration. You'll feel so much better when you're done—not just physically but mentally, spiritually, and emotionally too!

DEAR GOD, SOMETIMES I GET TOO BUSY AND DISTRACTED WITH ALL KINDS OF THINGS IN LIFE, AND I DON'T TAKE TIME TO PRAY OR EXERCISE. I KNOW I NEED BOTH OF THOSE THINGS REGULARLY TO HELP DEAL WITH STRESS AND WORRIES AND TO TAKE GOOD CARE OF MYSELF. PLEASE HELP ME TO FORM BOTH GOOD PHYSICAL HABITS AND GOOD PRAYER HABITS. AMEN.

Should We Keep on Sinning? Of Course Not!

Well then, should we keep on sinning so that God can show us more and more of his wonderful grace? Of course not!
ROMANS 6:1–2 NLT

Lots of people think it's no big deal to sin—making bad choices and disobeying God's Word. They just want to do what everyone else in the world says is popular and fun. And they might think that since Jesus saves people from sin, then why not sin however much you want and not worry about it? But no matter how much love and forgiveness God gives, sin always has consequences. So anyone who says they are a Christian but does not do their best to obey God will certainly have a lot of trouble in their lives.

Don't misunderstand—doing your best to obey God's Word does not mean a perfect life with zero trouble. But it does mean God helps you through every trouble and works everything out for good for those who love Him (Romans 8:28). So take good care of yourself and take a stand not to follow along with the world's popular ideas that sinning is fun and that God and His Word want to ruin all the "fun." God will bless and reward you for your loving commitment to Him and to doing your best to avoid sin like His Word instructs (Romans 6:11–14; 2 Timothy 2:22).

DEAR GOD, PLEASE HELP ME STAND STRONG AGAINST SIN. I WANT TO STAY COMMITTED TO LOVING AND FOLLOWING YOU AND YOUR PERFECT WAYS, ACCORDING TO YOUR WORD. AMEN.

Look for Fruit

[Jesus said,] "You will recognize them by their fruits."
MATTHEW 7:20 ESV

So, how do you really know if you're truly practicing good self-care in all the best ways? You'll produce good fruit! When someone chooses Jesus as Savior and has a true relationship with Him, they should be a bit like a good fruit tree. Just like a fruit tree is only healthy and growing well if it produces fruit, Christians are only healthy and growing well if we produce good fruit too—meaning the good deeds we do, the way we care for others, and the actions and habits that clearly show we love and follow Jesus and live by His Word. The good things we do are not what gain us salvation, but we were created to do good things. As we trust and follow Jesus, He brings us opportunities to do those good things (Ephesians 2:10). We will also have the fruit of the Spirit (Galatians 5:22–23)—love, joy, peace, patience, kindness, goodness, faithfulness, gentlenes, and self-control—evident in our lives.

So, take some time to think: What fruit are you producing, and how can you continue—and/or where do you need to take better care and make more fruit?

JESUS, PLEASE HELP ME TO TAKE GOOD CARE OF MYSELF WITH YOUR HELP AND ACCORDING TO YOUR WILL. PLEASE HELP ME PRODUCE ALL THE GOOD FRUIT YOU WANT ME TO. KEEP ME GROWING HEALTHY AND STRONG IN MY RELATIONSHIP WITH YOU. AMEN.

Our Best Earthly Self-Care Cannot Compare. . .

A single day in your courts is better than a thousand anywhere else! I would rather be a gatekeeper in the house of my God than live the good life in the homes of the wicked. For the Lord God is our sun and our shield. He gives us grace and glory. The Lord will withhold no good thing from those who do what is right. O Lord of Heaven's Armies, what joy for those who trust in you.

Psalm 84:10–12 NLT

Our very best self-care here on earth is just a glimpse of how wonderfully well God will take care of us in the perfect paradise of heaven forever someday. Nothing in this world is better than loving and worshipping and obeying the one true God. There is nowhere you can go that is better than being in His courts, within His kingdom. No one is worthy of relationship and worship like Him. No one is able to protect and provide for you like Him. No one loves you like Him. You are wonderfully blessed to be His child!

DEAR GOD, I PRAISE AND THANK YOU THAT I GET TO CALL YOU MY FATHER AND PROVIDER, MY FRIEND AND SAVIOR THROUGH JESUS CHRIST, MY COMFORTER AND HELPER THROUGH THE HOLY SPIRIT. ONE DAY WITH YOU IS TRULY BETTER THAN BEING ANYWHERE ELSE. I'M GRATEFUL THAT ALL OF MY DAYS ARE WITH YOU! AMEN.

Scripture Index

OLD TESTAMENT

NEW TESTAMENT

2 Timothy

Titus

Hebrews

James

1 Peter

1 John

Jude